CROTCH THINKING

A Memoir of Lust & Damage

DAVID THOMAS

ISBN 978-1-956696-36-3 (paperback)
ISBN 978-1-956696-38-7 (hardcover)
ISBN 978-1-956696-37-0 (digital)

Copyright © 2021 by David Thomas

All rights reserved. No part of this publication may be reproduced, distributed, or transmitted in any form or by any means, including photocopying, recording, or other electronic or mechanical methods without the prior written permission of the publisher. For permission requests, solicit the publisher via the address below.

Rushmore Press LLC
1 800 460 9188
www.rushmorepress.com

Printed in the United States of America

CONTENTS

Introduction v

Chapter 1: Repression. 1
Chapter 2: Crotch Thinking. 11
Chapter 3: Married Life 1: Children Having Children 25
Chapter 4: Professional Progress, Relational Strain 42
Chapter 5: Temptation Rules Again 56
Chapter 6: Married Life 2: Passionate Pleasure, Permanent Pain. . . 72
Chapter 7: Addiction Years 86
Chapter 8: A Child Won't Save Us 98
Chapter 9: Married Life 3: Getting It Right 111

Epilogue 121
Endnotes. 123

INTRODUCTION

For decades, news outlets periodically reported women's accusations of sexual abuse by prominent and powerful men. But none of these had the impact of the charges against Hollywood producer Harvey Weinstein.

In late 2017, the *New Yorker* and the *New York Times* detailed Weinstein's alleged misconduct, and in less than a month, eighty-four women had publically described instances of forced oral sex, Weinstein masturbating in front of them, naked demands for massages, and rape.[1]

A French actress told the *New Yorker* that Weinstein invited her to his hotel room in Cannes in 2010. "While she takes a call from a friend, he goes into his bathroom, where she hears the shower being turned on. She later says that he came out with an erection and demanded she lie on the bed. 'It was like a hunter with a wild animal,' she said. 'The fear turns him on.'"[2]

The sexual-allegation floodgates were opened, and media personalities Matt Lauer, Garrison Keillor, Charlie Rose, Kevin Spacey, and Dustin Hoffman; celebrity chef Mario Batali; NFL Hall of Famer Marshall Faulk; Senator Al Franken; and scores of other prominent men were publically accused. Many lost their jobs. By January 2018, millions of women in twenty countries had used #MeToo and #TimesUp to tell their stories.

Now, feminist author Mary Beard argues, "I would shift our gaze from celebrity harassment to the cases of 'ordinary' [people]. We are going to make progress only if we all pull together—from the casting couch to the factory floor."[3] This book responds to Beard's urging. It is an account of erection-driven life below the radar.

Crotch Thinking is a story about sexually propelled actions that cripple private lives in ways subtle enough to escape detection and display. The actions are insidious; although the damages individuals suffer are often serious and long-term, they are broadly understood and frequently dismissed as unfortunate features of normal contemporary life: Alcohol addiction. Lifelong struggle with weight. Prescription drug abuse. Promiscuity. Profound loss of self-esteem. Inability to trust. Depression.

All these happen behind the closed doors of family homes, Cub Scout parent gatherings, minimum-security jails, addiction counselor offices, and twelve-step meetings. When the events that precipitate them are noticed at all, they are dismissed with comments like "Boys will be boys." Or worse—"She asked for it." Victims are expected to suck it up and get on with their lives.

The conditions that create crotch thinking are physiological and cultural. Hormones happen to every human, and yet, even in 2019, little is done to empower young people to cope with the potent effects of hormones on immature thinking and feeling. In addition, while research has shown that medically accurate and comprehensive information about sexual health decreases risky behaviors, scare tactics, stigma, and shame continue to be hallmarks of formal and informal sexuality education.[4] So crotch thinking rages on.

Crotch Thinking reveals the intimate details of one baby boomer's life from his third year to his seventieth year. It illustrates the crucial importance, especially for men, of individual reflection on our sexuality—and of family, school, and community conversations about men's sexuality—by describing what happens when these conversations don't occur.

CHAPTER 1

Repression

I'm proud to be sitting on the big people's toilet. It's easy to tell from Mom's reaction that I'm doing something good. Most of the time, doing good is my main goal. True, I slithered under the dining room table where Scooter was napping and pulled his tail hard, but I was as shocked as everybody else by how he jumped, barked, and knocked over a chair. And his snarl scared me. That explosion rattled me as much as it angered Mom and Dad.

My point is I'm a fairly timid kid. I'm generally compliant, mostly because I'm usually a little scared of what might happen next. Remember that time I decided to run away from home a year or so after the toilet incident? I didn't get off our 60-by-120-foot city lot. Mom found me sitting in the swing that hangs from the rafters of the woodshed attached to our garage. Did Mom or Dad ever catch their preschool son with a knife? Throwing rocks at the windows? Even marking on the walls?

So when I'm on the toilet, I'm feeling pretty good about myself. I'm fiddling with my penis, but it's an absentminded fiddling. Then Dad pokes his head in the door to check on me. "If you play with that thing, it'll fall off," he snaps and scowls. "Knock it off!"

Dad's growl shames me, scares me, snaps me from my usual identity as do-good Dougie to morally suspect, shameful twerp.[5]

This happens partly because Dad can be scary. He's not a huggy guy. His long hours at our family's mom-and-pop grocery store, his naps, and his other activities mysterious to me keep us from spending much time together. Plus, Dad's the enforcer parent. When my sister and I get out of line, he threatens us with his razor strop, a pair of narrow, connected two-foot slabs of thick leather made for honing a straight-edge razor. It's a scary weapon, and he can make it pop really loud. The few times he actually uses it bruise our calves and bottoms. When he's really ticked off, we get rudely boosted down the hall to our bedrooms, one kick at a time. It's frightening, and it hurts.

At age three, I also don't know much about my body. When I run in the alley's dirt and gravel, my balance and coordination usually guarantee that I fall at least once. To keep from seeing double, I cock my head to look out of my right eye, and when Mom or Dad notices, they tell me to "Look straight" and "Stop squinting." I know next to nothing about what I've heard my folks call my "private parts."

So Dad's disapproval and stern warning sting. I'm just touching what feels good, but it's clear I've stepped over a line. Despite my pleasure, there's obviously something wrong with fingering there. I can tell from Dad's face and voice that this is serious business. Like when he violently kicks Scooter as the dog tries to rub himself on Dad's leg. Like when grown-ups talk about the hotel near the end of Main Street where a red light always burns over the entrance. Like my folks' disapproval of that *Saturday Evening Post* story about Mae West.

At the time, it doesn't occur to me that I've never seen Mom and Dad kissing, hugging, or even touching each other. But their physical disconnection significantly shapes the world I live in. Most nights after dinner, my older sister and I huddle around the Zenith console listening to *The Green Hornet*, *The Shadow*, or *The Jack Benny Program*. Dad usually sleeps in his chair—after 1951, in front of the television—and Mom occupies her sofa seat on the other side of the living room, darning socks, making a to-do list, and, late in the evening, smoking cigarettes and sipping a juice glass of jug wine.

During a visit to Aunt Helen and Uncle Robert, I see them kiss when he gets home from work. It looks like a regular thing. I notice Aunt Emmy and Uncle Fred comfortably standing side by side, each with one arm around the other. But even when Dad really blows Mom away on their wedding anniversary with sterling silver service for eight, she sheds tears of gratitude standing by herself on the other side of the dining table. They stand next to each other for the Brownie Hawkeye photo of the event, but Dad's delicately holding the tip of the blade of a silver knife in one hand and proudly pointing at it with the other while they both face the camera smiling. They don't touch or look at each other.

Mom and Dad's avoidance of intimate, personal touching, and what I later learn is sexual stuff, fits what many people in my world seem to prefer.

I enjoy playing at Grandma Thomas' house, for example, even though there's no hugging or cuddling there either. Lots of smiles and good times; not much physical affection. At Thanksgiving, we cram more than twenty aunts, uncles, and cousins into her bedroom-sized living and dining rooms. Genuinely happy greetings welcome everyone but no hugs. My sister, Lynn, and I have great fun playing with cousins Kathy, Frank, Amy, and Jack, but we don't wrestle, play tag, or do anything that would put us in physical contact. It's like most of the play spaces I'm in are shaped by the noes that lurk at their edges. The spaces are defined by what's prohibited, unspoken rules governing what can be done and what can be talked about.

When Lynn first tells me with great authority what happens "down there" when a man and a woman get together, it's clear that I'm supposed to keep it secret. My inarticulate preschool sense is that touch, closeness, private parts, and intimacy all go together and they need to be kept hidden because they're somehow shameful, dirty, and bad. I'm not sure whether the direction of my development happens despite or because of this climate. I know it is influential.

The Kinsey Institute reports common examples of two- to three-year-old children masturbating regularly. I'm not this highly sexed—or whatever it's called—but before the first grade, I do spend time thinking about girls, partly because family members enjoy hearing me talk about it. When I'm six, I boast to anyone who'll listen that I have sixteen girlfriends. I'm not sure who's counting or what "girlfriend" means, but I'm vividly aware of Nancy.

She is a spitting image, to me at least, of the young Shirley Temple. Artful makeup, glamour shots, movie posters, and feature film exposure all work their magic on me. Shirley Temple is so appealing! Her dazzling smile, vivacious bounce, effortless singing and dancing, quick wit, and adoring entourage draw me close and excite me. It never registers that she is more than a decade older than I am and that, by the time of my fixation, her early career has peaked. Woolworth and J.C. Penney still stock Shirley Temple dolls, phonograph records, mugs, hats, and dresses, so it's easy to make the comparison between Shirley and Nancy.

Nancy is also six and lives only two blocks away. When I look at her, all I see is adorable ringlets cascading over her ears and a dimpled smile that sparks me just like Shirley's posters do. I'm dazzled. I daydream about her. Think about her before I go to sleep. Our moms facilitate a pleasant play date or two, but predictably, our "relationship" doesn't go anywhere.

And the die is cast. Along with, and not always subordinate to slingshots, bikes, war games, and sneaking down the block to play in the millrace, girls, femininity, and attracting and being attracted to the other sex are important parts of my life from early on.

I don't actually date a girl until I take Vivian to the Fox Theatre for a Saturday matinee when we are both in the sixth grade. Recently, my wife told me that this was a little unusual too; she wasn't allowed to date until she was eighteen.

I spend secret time planning how to get my arm around Vivian while at the show. Observations of other couples and conversations with male friends help define this for me as the kind of intimacy that is not only desirable but also possible in the dark of the theater. It is exciting—sexually exciting, in fact—to think about. As it turns out,

I spend most of the film trying to get up my nerve, and my arm ends up around the back of the seat more than around Vivian.

As I get my growth spurt, my voice cracks and lowers, and my body sprouts hair in various places, more of my waking hours are focused on girls and sex. It's hard to appreciate today how many "this is good" and "this is bad" messages combine to create the repressive cultural context that frames this part of my development.

The Adventures of Ozzie and Harriet, Leave It to Beaver, and *Father Knows Best* define appropriate family relationships. Dad works while Mom keeps the family home, morals and values are simple and rigidly followed, and everybody is well behaved. Nobody talks about anything physical. Nobody masturbates, has an affair, or divorces, and outside of what might go on in the mysterious marriage bedroom, there is no deep kissing, petting, or advanced sexual activity.

Just one time during these years, I hear secondhand about a father and son in town who have a different set of rules. I am so caught up in the dominant narrative that their story shocks and disgusts me to the point that I don't want to hear any more about them, much less talk about them. I'm told that this dad would acknowledge his son's desire to masturbate and even hand him his handkerchief to come into. While they were in the car together! *Who does that?* I remember thinking. *Argh!*

I completely fail to notice that this family is doing part of exactly what needs to be done to make the culture's treatment of sexuality healthier. Dad and son are talking about masturbation, part of the natural process of sexual development that most adolescents experience—67 to 94 percent of males and 43 to 84 percent of females, according to a large-scale study by the National Survey of Sexual Health and Behavior.[6] At the time, I can't begin to realize that I should be learning from them rather than recoiling from them.

IUDs and the pill haven't been invented yet; few doctors are willing to prescribe a diaphragm for an unmarried woman; and condoms are kept out of sight behind drugstore counters, unavailable to young men or their dates, few of whom would have the nerve to buy one if they could. Abortions are available, I hear on the street, but only if you have a back-alley connection, travel far out of town, can pay the high cost, and are willing to take the serious risk of sterilization or other permanent injury.

The culture's accepted opinion about what young people should know about sex is expressed in the films that provide the only sex education in most schools. Separate male and female groups of students are chastened by films with such illustrative titles as *Boys Beware*, *How to Say No: Moral Maturity*, and *Girls Beware*, all chaperoned by faculty members who can't wait to get past this uncomfortable part of the school year. There are no educational discussions before or after the films. Just sidelong glances, nervous laughter, and crude jokes.

The cultural assumption is that the physical and moral parts of sex education happen at home, and this is far from the truth. A couple of my friends say their folks gave them a pamphlet from church that they were warned not to discuss with anybody. But it seems to my friends and me that our parents' generation knows only what they've learned from experience and that they are too uncomfortable to share it.

Late in life, I ask my folks if they ever talked with Lynn and me about sex, and Mom insists they did. Lynn and I don't remember it ever happening. When I'm in junior high, I snoop around my parents' bedroom while they're at work and discover a medically based, paperback sex manual hidden under a hat in one of my dad's hatboxes on the top shelf of their bedroom closet. I appreciate the information in the small sections that I can sneak the opportunity to read. The facts that Dad (and Mom?) have the book, that it is so carefully hidden, that I search their private spaces well enough to find it, and that neither the book nor my finding it is ever discussed speak volumes about the ignorance about and repression of sexuality in our family.

Since nobody is comfortable talking about sex publicly, it naturally is a prominent topic of most young people's private conversations, including those I have with friends.

Much of the lore that we exchange is laughable now. Masturbation can lead to mental illness. French-kissing can make her pregnant. If you pull out before you come, she'll never conceive. Girls think sex is dirty; only boys crave it. Oral sex is only for homosexuals.

Although *Playboy* starts publishing in the early 1950s, the cultural changes it helps create don't filter down to small towns like ours for a decade. This is part of what makes Mack's Shoeshine Shop a popular downtown place for us guys to visit. Its owner is locally known as "Mack the Swede," which says a lot about our town's racial climate.

Mack is a bona fide local character, an apparently forty-plus-year-old immigrant when I meet him, who looks and sounds the same from that day until his death four decades later. He's slender, not tall enough to be intimidating, mostly bald, and almost always smiling. His English is what my folks call "broken" but not so much that I can't understand him. Mack's shop and Dad's grocery are separated by only an accountant, a photographer, a tavern, and a hotel lobby, so they're business friends. Dad's proud enough of me that at some point he parades me in front of most of his downtown friends, so I get to be one of the kids who knows Mack well enough to visit his place.

When the six raised chairs in his shop are empty, Mack can be seen cleaning and blocking the hats that every man wears at the time. But he is usually energetically shining shoes and carrying on at least a couple of conversations. His leisure activity appears to consist mainly of weekly train trips to his "girlfriends" ninety miles East. For these occasions, he dudes up in a purple silk suit, custom cut for him by his tailor back home in Stockholm.

Mack has the good marketing sense to provide titillation for his all-male clientele with an endless stream of off-color jokes, salty language, and dozens of pulp adult comics featuring women's ample bottoms, larger-than-life breasts, and eagerness for sex. Fortunately for us horny boys, Mack also has an almost grotesquely large right bicep, developed by the vigorous buffing of decades of shoes. He enjoys impressing us by flexing and wiggling this muscle, and not only do we get a kick out of this display, but it also gives us an excuse to drop by so we can steal looks at his collection of soft porn.

Like all groups of twelve- to seventeen-year-old boys, we who frequent Mack's regale each other with stories about who has "done it" with whom, which girls are loose and which aren't, well-hidden parking spots close to town, and who's gotten knocked up. The absence of healthy, well-informed outlets means that most of what is passed around in these conversations is exaggerated, physiologically inaccurate, lascivious, and thoroughly misogynist, especially because the world around us forces it into the shadows. I often feel as if my body is under the control of hormones that course through me unbidden, and the culture I am immersed in heaps guilt and shame on where these chemicals lead my feelings and thoughts.

The patterns young people follow seem silly in hindsight, but at the time they are the water we fish swim in. By grade seven, boys and girls are expected to begin to pair up. A few suffering from what doctors at the time call "delayed puberty" aren't interested or capable until they get to high school, but by freshman year, almost every kid is in the game. The two or three I know who turn out to be LGBT stay deep in the closet.

The high school's activity programming—athletics, class plays, open house, dances, band concerts—all include openings for steadies to spend time together, and for those who are temporarily single to scope out and get close to potential partners.

Adults seem to believe that dances, mostly sock hops, can provide enough opportunities for light necking to keep the teenage pregnancy rate reasonable and minimize the amount of underage drinking. Dances happen after almost every game throughout the year, and the Rollerdrome outdoes its school competition with a sanded floor, upgraded sound, and a large disco ball that flashes multihued spots and beams over ceiling, walls, and floor. Its Friday and Saturday night dances draw couples and cruising singles from all over the county.

Rollerdrome dances are especially appealing, because we can be sure that no teachers are around as chaperones, and the place has enough of a young-people-only vibe to keep most parents away. The sound system is also better than any school can afford for its gym. Management keeps the lights low, and seating around the perimeter of the oval floor provides space to spend private time with your date. Seats are theatre style and bolted to the floor, which challenges serious snuggling. But it feels private. Both the fast and the slow music of this decade—by Elvis, Pat Boone, Bobby Darin, Gogi Grant, Johnnie Ray, The Dell Vikings—is for couples rather than lines or groups, so one-on-one connections are encouraged.

Guys have culturally sanctioned ways of talking about our fantasy life: first base (deep kissing), second base (petting), third base (genital manipulation), and home run (intercourse, usually called fucking or some euphemism like "doing it"). Young men work toward running the bases. Young women effectively draw and erase lines prohibiting and permitting these activities.

Truth be told, no responsible adult is in charge of what is available for us kids to do. But it looks from the inside as if our lives are supposed to consist of school, family, dating, and enough part-time work to pay for gas. The 30 percent of us looking toward college pay more attention to high school than those heading for work in their dad's gas station, the farm, or the cannery. Some families enjoy real togetherness in church and on vacations. Cultural expectations lead the others to maintain at least a facade of normalcy, and this also requires a measure of the kids' time and attention. Work is important for those already starting on their blue-collar life trajectory, but for many of us, jobs are fungible, so long as we get enough hours to make enough to meet our needs. Since gas is a quarter a gallon, burgers thirty-five cents, and soft serve starts at a dime, this doesn't take much.

For most of us in high school, dating activities appear to be haphazardly constructed to give us practice, ideally dry runs, at being in a grown-up, long-term, monogamous relationship. But, at least for myself and the guys I talk with, the endgame of marriage and family is completely out of sight and out of mind. We're definitely not thinking about life insurance, a mortgage, furniture payments, or babies, diapers, and high chairs. We are much more narrowly focused on coping with hormone-fueled desires and improving our base-running success. When talking with friends, almost all of us have to exaggerate how well we're doing in order to maintain respectability.

There are no opportunities for honest, well-informed conversations about sex, not at home, in school, at church, or in organizations like Boy Scouts, Little League, or the Boys and Girls Club. Instead, cultural pressures from parenting manuals, teacher education programs, youth organizations, and the increasingly influential media—radio, movies, comic books, television—proscribe even the use of such words as "breast," "petting," "masturbation," and certainly "penis" and "vagina." Serious social pressure blocks talk about sex, and damaging cultural punishment happens to those who violate these expectations. Being a kid in the 1950s is not for the faint of heart.

CHAPTER 2

Crotch Thinking

A pattern begins about this time when my default option becomes thinking with my crotch. I continue to be a generally conforming rule follower, appreciated by some teachers, and a potential leader, but I clearly fall in the 54 percent of males that Kinsey says think about sex every day.[7] As I move into adolescence, I recognize a pattern of slowly growing interest that I attribute mainly to hormones, an interest that either peaks in orgasm or is diverted by intense physical activity, cold temperatures, illness, or significant stress. When one or more of these happen, the drive for sexual satisfaction that I'm experiencing lessens, at least temporarily.

The opposite happens when a thought, smell, sight, or physical touch triggers an erection. Then I experience what Robin Williams described: "God gave men both a penis and a brain, and only enough blood to run one at a time."[8] Masters and Johnson put this point scientifically when they explain that the engorgement of blood vessels in the male "that results in full penile erection serves in effect as a transformer mechanism by which the effectiveness of initial sexual stimuli is increased many times in the male's consciousness ... the male's sensual focus usually is directed solely to the full, tense demand of the erect penile organ."[9]

If you're a guy, I know you've experienced this. Unless you're asleep, an erection amplifies whatever sexual stimuli created it to the point where your sensual focus is directed "solely to the full, tense demand of the erect penile organ." This is what I mean by crotch thinking. Brain thinking recedes into the background or disappears. When an erection occurs, most men are intensely focused by the demand we're experiencing, the "full, tense demand" to achieve orgasm. And in this aroused condition, as researchers also say, men are willing to engage in risky behavior to achieve orgasm.[10] This is why crotch thinking is dangerous. This is why it can hurt others.

I'm not a pedophile, rapist, sex addict, or stalker, and I'm pretty sure I'm not a sex abuser. I've performed worthwhile actions for individuals and organizations. I've been recognized for some of them. Where sex is concerned, I know that "No" means no.

I also understand that human behavior is complex, and almost no actions have a single cause. Yet I know that at crucial times in my life I've acted while thinking with my crotch and it's hurt people. Myself, for one. And others, as you'll read. Many of the hurts stayed private. You won't find press coverage of the damage, and this is part of what makes it insidious. Some of these hurts are little known, and if known, are considered unfortunate, unavoidable, or even normal. Nonetheless, they can be ruinous. Although the results of crotch thinking often remain below the radar, they can be both widespread and long-term.[11]

Like everyone in my high school, I do pay attention to topics other than sex. School life is becoming easier, which means that teachers' evaluations of my intelligence and capabilities are getting more positive. Lynn begins deferring subtly to me as the smarter sibling, even though she's older; Dad is increasingly boastful about his son; and although I suspect that Mom's insightful enough to know that a second shoe will eventually drop, she can't help but smile and cut slack.

My serious interest in things mechanical keeps me from always thinking about sex. In high school, this mechanical curiosity is fueled by the vice principal, Mr. Frame. He publicly refuses to let his son Bob own a car before he graduates, because, Mr. Frame insists, when high school boys get cars, their grades go down. Bob's plight solidifies my determination to prove Mr. Frame wrong by finding cheap wheels and maintaining my honor roll grades.

At this age, I'm as interested in the head bolt tightening pattern on the engine of a Ford flathead as the threat that parallax poses to the accurate reading of the slide rule required in my physics and chemistry classes. None of the smartest kids in my class share this level of enthusiasm for mechanics. They don't seem to get it that a car is both an end in itself—getting greasy to effect a fix you can immediately observe is satisfying—and a means to the greater end of having access to a mobile platform for making out. Dad unwittingly supports my project by telling the authorities that he needs me to haul groceries to the store from the wholesaler four miles away in the next town. So without the obstacle of Driver's Ed., I get my driver's license at fifteen and find a 1950 Ford that the owner of Dave's Chevron sells me for $250.

Thinking with my crotch, though, never really goes away. The contextualizing frame or pervasive musky aroma surrounding the multidimensional developmental mash-up I experience intensifies my normal preteen angst. It feels as if I'm inhabited against my will by a life force that narrows my attention like the performance expectations around an important exam and sharpens it like too much caffeine. Sex is on my mind, waking and sleeping. I can concentrate enough to study successfully, remember to change the oil in my car, and keep from getting fired at work. But time with women shares at least equal importance with school, work, and machines, and my spare and fantasy time thoughts are virtually all sex related.

The stress is intensified by my dim but regularly reinforced realization that cultural forces continue to render the whole sexual life focus untalkaboutable, except among the guys. Sexual dreams happen for what seems like no reason, and when they do, erotic longing mixes with guilt and shame picked up from implicit and explicit moral forces all around me.

Surprising erections sharpen my sense of not being in control. I begin investing considerable thought and energy in ways to hide the too-frequent bulges that pop up at inopportune times. Like when I join half a dozen high school friends in the back seat of a '53 Plymouth—no seat belts, of course—girls on the laps of the guys. I've never been particularly attracted to Patricia, who is perched on my knees, but past or present romantic interest is obviously irrelevant to my body. *Can she feel me poking her bottom?* I worry all the way to the Burger Barn.

Before high school dates, I don one or sometimes two athletic supporters—jockstraps that I've been required to purchase in order to turn out for junior varsity basketball. They help a little, like bands compressing the developing breasts of an embarrassed teen female. But I still recall a necking and petting session in my car with Karen when she abruptly grabs my well-clothed erection and asks, "What's this? Do you have a knife in your pocket?" I probably should have taken it as a compliment, but at the time, I am awkwardly speechless. I wish I'd been able to come up with a smooth and sexy response like "I'll give you forty-five minutes to let go of that." At least she didn't add, "Or are you just happy to see me?"

I don't mean to place all the blame for my sexual immaturity on outside forces. But the combination of lack of information, family secrecy patterns, mixed-message dances and other adult-supervised activities, exaggerations from friends, cultural guilt and shame, and the seemingly inexorable, hormone-fueled push toward sexual thoughts and feelings do leave me with the sense that, in these matters, I have a lot less control than I wish I did. Everybody knows not to spit on the floor. You do basically what your parents tell you, even when you don't want to. You come to a full stop before turning right. But sexual desires, fantasies, images, and bodily responses happen whether you intend, plan, and want them to or not.

These pressures complicate my four high school years of fairly active dating. Along the way, teasing from girls like Kelly undercuts my confidence as a player by calling attention to non-macho handicaps of mine like the space between my large, protruding front teeth that was caused, according to my mom and sister, by too much thumb-sucking. "Kiss me, buckteeth! My tonsils itch!" Kelly regularly calls, and although I try to laugh it off each time, she's a popular enough leader in the "socie" clique that the wound stings my adolescent psyche. I am engaged just enough in typically male pursuits to make the cut from gay to straight, but since I don't shoot deer or game birds and am too scrawny for football, too short for varsity basketball, and too visually challenged for baseball—my only competitive sport is tennis—the space I fill at high school is testosterone-light.

I do manage to maintain a serially monogamous life in multimonth "going steady" relationships with Laura, Sharon, and Peg. Each is bright; two are noticeably attractive; and Peg is a school star. There is no intense sexual activity with any of them, but not because I don't push in that direction, especially with Peg. We're together over two years in high school and get close enough that our parents develop a friendship that lasts after Peg breaks up with me. Although she is okay with extended necking sessions, she is especially adept at nonverbally saying, "That's enough." Both Sunday school and family influences compel me to respect her wishes. I don't like it, but, as I said, I do understand that "No" means no.

I also feel "blue balls" frustrated, because of another set of unspoken expectations about sexual activity that shape the lives of males my age—and a few females. The picture painted by what's around me is that there is a normal trajectory that everybody close to my age is moving along—going around the bases—where one level of sexual activity naturally leads to the next, and if that one is agreeable to both parties, we go on to what follows, and then to the next, culminating in orgasm. Tellingly, the end game as I understand it is orgasm, not lovemaking or even intercourse. Like I'm just using her vagina to masturbate. Focused on me, not us.

I'm not sex-crazed enough to ignore the place of love in all the physical intimacy I wish for, fantasize about, and furtively plan. But in high school, is it really possible for a guy to understand this topic? How much does the development of our forebrains actually permit?

I notice that popular songs are all about love, so I briefly reason that they might help untangle this moral-physical-emotional mess. But no. The lyrics of hits like the Everly Brothers' "All I Have to Do Is Dream" and Perry Como's "Catch a Falling Star" are only good for mood setting. And although the title of the Fleetwoods' "Come Softly to Me" is cleverly ambiguous, this song isn't informative either. Buried in a surplus of "Dahm dahm, dahm do dahm ooby doos," this group pines, "Please hold, hold me so tight, all through, all through the night," which suggests something pretty clearly but offers absolutely no practical help. The same is true of other hits like Domenico Modungo's "Volare," Ricky Nelson's "Poor Little Fool," and even Frankie Avalon's "Venus." Despite its promising title, there are not many places you can go with "Venus, if you do, I promise that I always will be true, I'll give you all the love I have to give, as long as we both shall live."

Say what?

A Sunday school lesson I dimly recall left me knowing about the "love chapter" of 1 Corinthians, and my budding commitment to scholarship motivates me to study the relevant text to try to make some sense out of what I am feeling toward Laura, Sharon, and Peg and what I am occasionally sensing from them. On the one hand, I can relate to the "love is patient and kind ... it is not arrogant or rude" admonitions. Since I've been raised in a family with a moral base and have been a fairly decent kid—no arrests for shoplifting; no fights, school suspensions, or expulsions; only in serious trouble with my folks a few times—I understand not "to rejoice at wrong." Since my life has been pretty privileged, I'm a whole lot less clear about "bears all things, believes all things, hopes all things, endures all things." I also notice the chasm between "Love never ends" and what I know about the frequency of divorce. The big problem though, one that I see today and I certainly didn't see then, is the "now we see in a mirror dimly, but then face to face" part. I'm in the dark, because, at the time, I don't know what I don't—and can't—know. A blind man in a bomb factory.

So I blunder forward, equipped with a life-threatening and life-creating weapon I neither understand nor fear, propelled by what feels like a river current powered by gravity and fluid kinetics in a direction that has the potential to scramble, enrich, or cripple me and people around me. My adolescent rejection of my dad's occupation gets me fired from my job as grocery store bag boy, but I hold down other age-appropriate jobs as newspaper carrier, part-time school janitor, swimming teacher, and tire installer. I earn honor roll grades in classes that, for the most part, I enjoy. I serve on student council, am elected junior class president, run for student body president and lose, represent my school at Boys' State, win the election for senior class president, have leading roles in a couple of school plays, and am voted "Most Likely to Succeed" in my high school graduating class.

These accomplishments delight my folks, make it easier to find part-time jobs, position me to plan for college, and burnish my identity at school and in our small town as a potential leader. But nobody in my cheering section suspects the degree to which three interests take up the lion's share of the space in my life: school, cars, and sex.

School stays pretty prominent. Dad started his college career at our town's community college. He excelled in the natural sciences to the point where Dad and his chemistry instructor planned for him to become a physician. The Great Depression of the 1930s abruptly put an end to this plan, but it didn't dampen Dad's enthusiasm for the school. I am frankly scared at the prospect of attending the state's premier institution, and scholarship support I receive at high school graduation encourages me to invest my first two college years in the low-cost, low-risk option offered by our two-year college.

It's easy to get engaged in both classes and co-curricular programs here. I learn a transformative lesson first term in Mr. Ristuben's English class. High school advisers warned me that my B+ to A- grades in high school would be C-level scores in college.

This becomes my operating expectation. Then, when Mr. Ristuben explains that a major part of his final will be an in-class theme on one of three topics he shares with the class, I realize that I can prepare for this part of the test by outlining and memorizing the main points of a theme on each of the three. I ace the test and the class, and my success in this course and others begins to convince me that college might not be as tough as I've been told. The rest of this year and the next eight, I learn that higher education gets easier as you go along, because you get better and better at classes that focus more and more on what interests you.

Late fall term, I pursue my plan to attend law school by interviewing three local attorneys about their work. I learn that all three are much more interested in winning than in justice, and my naive idealism recoils. Partly because of my law school plans, I've become active in debate and forensics. These activities introduce me to thorough research and to engagement with thinking about such complex questions as whether Congress should have the power to overturn decisions of the Supreme Court, and whether the US should enact a program of universal health insurance. I also begin to see that there is a profession for people who want to earn a living with research and scholarship, and I shift my professional plan from law to the goal of becoming a university professor.

Since I'm a relatively big fish in a definitely small pond, other co-curricular activities are attractive. I enjoy being secretary for the Circle K service club, producing a column for the school weekly, and being part of Phi Theta Kappa, the national community college honorary. I'm successful enough academically to be identified in this year's annual as "Freshman Scholar with High Honors." Four of us in debate and forensics travel with our coach "out West" to Utah for a national tournament, the longest trip I've ever taken. Then, Circle K makes it possible for me and two friends to attend the service club's international convention in Toronto, a real journey.

I replace the Ford with a '51 Chevy that's already been customized with frenched '55 Chevy headlights, '54 Chevy taillights, a nose and deck job, electric doors, and twelve-inch glasspack mufflers that give it a distinctive and loud sound. My friend Jim's folks agree to let us overhaul the Chevy's engine in their carport, and after we've dismantled the engine, had the valves ground, replaced piston rings and crankshaft bearings, and installed new gaskets, plugs, points, rotor, distributor cap, and fluids, I have it painted Thunderbird Bronze and name it Racketeer. As planned, this ride doesn't hurt my efforts on life focus number three.

First Haley and then Ann get my attention when I graduate from high school. Haley and I spend almost every day together during the holidays, but we find we can't sustain this level of investment in each other. Ann's a year younger, really smart, and the daughter of my history teacher and forensics coach, and we connect closely. Her parents are welcoming for several months. I get invited on a spring camping trip with their family, during which I learn that her dad actually puts ketchup on french fries. This delicious culinary practice sticks with me today.

Unfortunately, her dad's support wanes after ten months of Ann and I spending increasing amounts of time together. He decides, I learn later, that the risk of our becoming sexually active is too great, and he insists that she break it off. I'm crushed.

One effect of my commitment to monogamy is that I go deep, if you'll pardon the expression. I commit to my dating and "steady" relationships emotionally and intellectually, more fully the more I mature. I also continue to push our sexual engagement, although Ann stops me at second base. I still have thoughts that we might be destined to be together. Her dad's concerns are probably well grounded, and the effect of our breakup on me is pretty severe.

Since high school, my dating MO has been to ask out a young woman whom I hear is interested in me. I don't make the first move. This strategy has the obvious advantage of protecting my fragile male identity, and it serves me pretty well. Soon after breaking up with Ann, I get the word that Ellen has noticed me. In my needy condition, I rebound toward Ellen like a ball off a wall.

I have no idea how consequential this is. Ellen is half a year younger than me, moderately well-known and well respected, even though she lives on the other side of the tracks. In our town, it isn't exactly "the wrong side of the tracks," but the best new homes aren't being built near her family's place on Washburn Street. Ellen and her twin brother, Don, live with their stay-at-home mom and their dad, a baker at a local supermarket. Their family is half a step below ours socioeconomically in a town where many families are a step or two above us both.

Ellen is an above-average student, sings in a select women's ensemble, chaired her class's junior prom, and was on the prom court. She's also a natural athlete. She plays shortstop on what is called the "girls'" softball team, and on one of our early dates at the bowling alley, she rolls 224 to my 108.

She is pleasant looking, has a beautiful smile and considerable grace, and is known among the guys for her well-developed breasts. Clearly at least D-cup, we decide. She is several inches shorter than me, and one of the ways I court her is to concentrate on looking into her eyes rather than down her chest when we slow dance. I mean to communicate that I respect her, which I do. I also mean to build trust. I do appreciate her sweetness and authenticity. And I'm thinking with my crotch. I spend many of my reflective and fantasy moments greedily envisioning what it'll be like to get my hands on her bare breasts.

The bowling date I mentioned is not the highlight of our early relationship, but we have fun together at dances and outings with friends. Days of foreplay, I hope. Ellen's twin brother is considerably more of a player than either his sister or me. Don sports an Elvis ducktail, wears his pants low, and knows how to twist, shimmy, inhale cigarette smoke, drink beer, and pick up willing women. His talents and activities have paved the way for permissiveness by Ellen's parents, a condition that is enhanced by the fact that her dad works from four in the morning to early afternoon and sleeps most of the day.

Like most eighteen-year-old women, Ellen is also more mature sexually than her nineteen-year-old boyfriend.[12] I'm too focused on my own desires to notice that she is less driven to lust by hormones and more encouraged by them down the road of mate selection and nesting. Marriage and family are comfortable topics for her, and, like most guys I run around with, they are the farthest things from my mind. Without either of us realizing how different we are in this way, Ellen and I progress around the bases.

I can't believe my good fortune. As always, I mindlessly push forward sexually, and, as never happened before, she's less resistant than other dates have been. Her breasts are every bit as exciting as I thought they'd be—even more. When she ends up nude in the Chevy's front seat, I can hardly breathe. Condom use never enters my mind. Passion propels us together, and I can tell it's the first time for both of us.

Our interlude is embarrassingly short, and since the Chevy is our only really private space, our liaisons continue to be furtive, mostly unplanned, mutual passion without reflection, at least on my part. I've been fantasizing about, wishing for, planning, strategizing, and then disappointed and frustrated about sex for so long—almost a third of my life—that the fact that it's happening, that I'm having sex regularly, is difficult to believe. I don't know about Ellen, but I don't tell anybody. I don't even brag to the most prominent players I know. In fact, I hardly think about it in between times, as if reflection might make it go away.

I also don't think about what comes next or where this activity might eventually lead. What's after a home run? "If sex, then engaged to be married?" Never enters my mind. "If intercourse, then permanency?" Not considered. This is obviously another feature of thinking with my crotch. My future focus doesn't extend beyond the tip of my penis or the recovery time after my last orgasm.

Ellen and I have just enough sense to talk briefly about when "the rhythm method" says we should abstain. In these pre-Google days, though, neither of us really understands the biological principles underlying this approach to contraception. It never occurs to me to do some careful research. Or to explore what's behind the drugstore counter.

Her fantasies very likely feature a cottage with a picket fence, smiling rug rats, and happily ever after. Mine are much more bodily, graphic, and crude. Oral sex. New positions. Twice in one night.

Predictably, but for me only in hindsight, she tells me in early January 1961 that she is pregnant. We both know I'm the only one who could be the father.

I'm halfway through my second year of community college. Three scholarships are paying my tuition and fees, and I'm planning where to transfer to complete my bachelor's degree. I am beginning to get increasingly comfortable in college, and my life plan is getting clearer. It requires three degrees beyond the associate of arts that I'm currently pursuing.

Ellen's pregnancy—this is before men acknowledged that it is *our* pregnancy—challenges my planning, but, and this is another testament to my lack of serious reflection, not as drastically as it could have. Each of us has a scary meeting with our parents, and both sets are saddened, worried, and supportive. My dad's mad at Ellen, because he thinks she's intentionally trapped me. Mom convinces him that it takes two to tango.

Ellen and I briefly consider terminating the pregnancy by having her take quinine, a malaria medicine that we hear on the streets can cause a spontaneous abortion. We agree that I'll ask my chemistry professor about it, and he directs me to literature that details quinine's ineffectiveness and life-threatening side effects. So, early on, we agree that we are going to have this baby.

Given my immaturity and the way I stumbled into this relationship, it wouldn't have been surprising for me to find all kinds of reasons and devise various ways to stay single. This isn't what happens. I'm grown-up enough to understand my responsibility, especially given that Ellen seems to be a pleasant enough partner. We agree we'll get married, quietly and soon, and I'll continue going to school. I have a summer job lined up managing the swimming pool in a nearby town, and the scholarships make me optimistic about future college funding. Neither of us dwells on future challenges or threats, and we agree to continue on my life plan, one step at a time.

I can't say what Ellen is feeling, other than fear, but I know that I enjoy being with her, care about and for her, and realize that she and I are in this together. I haven't yet solved the love problem, and I fail completely to understand the enormous downside of marrying someone you don't know how to love. But the pregnancy pushes this issue aside, and crotch thinking isn't sophisticated. My parents reluctantly help to locate a minister eighty miles away who is willing to perform what can only be called a shotgun wedding.

Ellen and I shop for inexpensive rings and order a corsage for her. Seven of us—her parents, my parents, the two of us, and Grandma Thomas—drive to the brief ceremony on the afternoon of February 11, 1961. It's held in the small chapel of a neighborhood church. The seven of us and the pastor are the only ones in the room. There is no premarital counseling. Ellen and I have no input into the vows. I like what the minister says about the symbolism of wedding rings, and this is the extent to which the ceremony feels special to me.

My parents are grimly supportive. They seem to be biting their tongues and hoping against hope. Grandma Thomas cries what strike me as something other than just wedding tears. Afterward, Ellen and I drive another seventy miles to the coast for a weekend honeymoon.

Since we're now married and she's already pregnant, my hope is for the weekend to be spent mostly in bed. This hope fails to acknowledge how immature we are, individually and as a couple. Thirty minutes or so after having sex, I am embarrassed to walk to the bathroom in front of her, because, since we're naked and in bed together, I already have another erection. Of course, neither of us is willing or able to talk about what's happening. *Plus ça change, plus c'est la meme chose.*

The next morning, we get a glimpse of how we appear to others when the server at breakfast includes with our sausage and eggs a small wedge of "honeymoon salad"—lettuce alone. We walk through the shops and visit the studio where my sister's favorite watercolorist offers his iconic ocean scenes. After lunch, we head for the beach, only to be forced back to the car by gale force winds driving cold rain that stings our exposed skin and foreshadows harsh realities we'll face for the next several years.

CHAPTER 3

Married Life 1: Children Having Children

Back from the beach, Ellen and I move into her upstairs bedroom on Washburn Street. "Move in" exaggerates, since we have no wedding gift toaster, bath towels, dishes, or tableware and no furniture. She makes room in one drawer of her old dresser for the clothes I bring, and I start learning how to sleep through each night's train noise and how not to upset the life rhythms of her dad, her twin brother, and her mom.

Most just-married couples have gone through months of wedding planning, couple's counseling, prenuptial parties, a memorable public ceremony, posing for professional photography, a family- and friend-filled reception, tearful toasts and dances, gift opening, thank-you writing, and a honeymoon that may involve a trip of a lifetime. These events make their marriage a punctuating event in their lives, an experience that creates a *before* and *after* in the couple's history. Ellen and I have none of this. My before and after is limited to where I lay my head and the newly relaxed secrecy of our sexual activity.

I feel as if I'm in a steady-girlfriend-with-benefits or "really serious" man-woman relationship. But I don't feel "married" or "partnered for life." Even though I'm sleeping with Ellen every night, our being together gets subordinate attention in my life, compared with my efforts to be a good student.

As a result, when a doctor's appointment in April culminates in a painful cauterization in the physician's office, I head home to recuperate—which for me means to my parents' house. I spend the afternoon moaning on my folks' couch and later learn how much Ellen's feelings are hurt by my choice. Her complaints puzzle me. As I mentioned, she's been thinking about marriage and family much longer than I have, and I don't yet get it that she and I are supposed to be the primary relationship in my life, not me and my folks. If I were in love with her, this probably wouldn't be a problem. But for me, that isn't part of being married. It's about sex and doing what's right, not love.

Both Ellen and I are taking classes at the community college, although another difference between us is that she's not on the kind of academic trajectory that pulls and pushes me. We're visible enough as a couple that the school features us at the Sweetheart Ball with ersatz crowns and a special dance. The full-page picture in this year's annual shows us as a smiling couple, Ellen on my lap, and me sporting a prominent zit on my chin. Children about to have a child.

Everybody knows why we're married, and nobody teases or ridicules either of us; this would require some hypocrisy on the part of other shotgun-wed couples, and, more importantly, it would require talking about the untalkaboutable. There are no pregnancy or childbirth classes for us to attend individually or together. Ellen's baby bump grows, we both study for the courses we're taking, and I serve as president of the Circle K service club, continue to write a column for the school newspaper, take photographs and help produce the newspaper and annual, and travel several weekends with the debate team.

My debate involvement connects me with students and faculty at four-year schools in the region, including the professor who chairs the speech department at a Presbyterian college two hundred miles away. Stories I continue to hear about the huge and impersonal state university convince me to focus my application interests on smaller, private schools, and the school's Professor Knutson makes my decision easy when he funnels a full-tuition debate and forensics scholarship my way. This grant, summer earnings, and the scholarships awarded me when I graduated from high school will just about cover expenses, which is a good thing, since neither set of parents is financially able to help much. I'm excited about the opportunity.

After the community college graduation ceremony, Ellen and I drive forty miles South for my summer job. We move our clothes and few belongings into a thirty-five-dollar-a-month furnished apartment three blocks from the community swimming pool I'm managing.

The dark and deteriorating ground-floor unit smells musty, and we share it with mice that clatter behind the kitchen drawers at night and leave droppings for Ellen to sweep up each day. Mostly, though, we appreciate this three-month opportunity to get to know each other, begin experiencing life as partners, and cope with the challenges of having sex during pregnancy. Although our relationship changes some, our conversation patterns don't; there's more talk about where I'll go trout fishing before work than there is about future challenges or our sex lives. I continue to focus more on work than on being married.

It's not that I ignore Ellen. I haven't yet learned the meaning of the word "codependent," so I have no sense of the downside of my eagerness to make things okay for Ellen and our unborn baby. Without really making them a top priority, I express care about her comfort, help around the house, listen to her concerns, and generally try to be supportive. Kind of like being nice to a good friend. The two of us are also grateful that our marriage and pregnancy insulate me from the Vietnam draft, which has already claimed Ellen's brother and several of our friends. I like having a regular and legitimate sexual partner, and I think Ellen does too. We enjoy playing a version of "house." Mine is much more superficial than hers—one more manifestation of crotch thinking.

Ellen is healthy and relatively comfortable the whole time. She doesn't like it when the temperature reaches ninety and I'm at the pool all afternoon, but she has no problems with morning sickness or mood swings. Ellen tells me that her mom was the same way with each of her four pregnancies. During a visit to her home, Ellen's mom comments casually, "It seems like I got pregnant every time Fred hung his pants on the bedstead." Both she and my mom begin easing into the "soon we'll be grandmas" stage. The dads, not so much.

At Ellen's August 7 doctor's appointment, we're told that the baby's on its way and Ellen better get to the hospital. After seeing her into a wheelchair at the front desk, I frantically jump into the Chevy and start racing the four miles to Washburn Street to tell the parents and get "the bag" we've packed. Halfway there on the gravel back road, I'm stopped by a local cop who responds to my "We'rehavingababy! We'rehavingababy!" shrieks with an understanding smile and advice to take it easy the rest of the way.

In 1961, expectant dads aren't allowed anywhere near the surgical suites where babies are born, so I pace the maternity ward waiting room just like I've seen in the movies. Typically for first babies, labor's a little long, but early the next morning, I get the news that we have a healthy baby girl. I'm relieved that it's over, grateful it went well, and completely unaware of how much more my life is about to change.

The first time I see Ellen and our little girl, I'm relieved that everybody's okay and completely charmed. Ellen is ecstatic and glowing. The only leftover from labor is a little fatigue. But she's clearly in her element. Born to be a mom. I don't fully get it at the time, but even though I'm a compulsive helper, I'm going to have a dedicated and competent partner raising this child. In fact, as parents go, I'm never going to have to be first or best. Ellen will have it handled. I can do my own thing, I superficially conclude.

The doctor and various lay savants around us predicted a boy, so Ellen and I recall our conversations about how the male name we'd chosen could be adapted if necessary. Kent becomes Kelsie, and our little one begins, for us, to take on sparkling features we associate with her name.

Before leaving the hospital, we can see that Kelsie has some distinctive qualities that will stay with her at least through her preschool and primary years. As we put it then, "She's a Gerber baby," every bit as terminally cute as the dimpled darling that graces the jars of Gerber baby food. Of course, every newborn is treated as "Sooo cute!" Yet I've seen both boy and girl babies that really aren't. Kelsie really is. She's worth all the Kodachrome that's spent on her by parents, family, and friends.

Classes start soon, so we've only got a couple of weeks to introduce Kelsie to the two sets of grandparents and our local extended families. Everybody's excited and supportive, and Kelsie charms all of them as much as she delights her mom and me. During one of our circulating visits, Kelsie ends up in the arms of my twentysomething cousin, Bob, who obviously has no experience with little ones. He sits in a rocker, nervously and rapidly propelling it back and forth while holding his trunk upright to keep Kelsie still. Doesn't want to break her, he says. The teasing laughter's fun.

Too soon for us, Ellen, Kelsie, and I transport our few belongings to a unit in married student housing on the college's lower campus. We're assigned to one of eight duplexes built for post-WWII vets and their families. Ours has three bedrooms and features brown battleship linoleum everywhere, a fuel oil space heater, skin-thin walls, drafty windows, a cramped kitchen with apartment-sized cookstove, a noisy steel shower, and a central courtyard of dirt and grass with slide and swings. The rent here is also thirty-five dollars a month. Most units contain kids, so community's easy to build.

Mainly by Ellen and Kelsie, though. I'm busy with classes and activities like Blue Key, Pi Kappa Delta, drama, and forensics. About a dozen times during the school year, I travel with the debate squad over long weekends to tournaments a state or two away. Junior year, my debate partner and I are invited to the national tournament at West Point, and senior year, the squad takes the train to Illinois for the national Pi Kappa Delta competition. Junior year, I also win the title role in the spring play.

An incident during play rehearsal provides a glimpse into the continuing immaturity of Ellen's and my relationship. The script emphasizes my character's early happiness partly by showing him and his wife blissfully kissing. When Ellen discovers this, she insists that I tell the director I can't follow this stage direction. The classmate playing my wife is attractive, and Ellen tells me that she can't stomach the idea of me kissing her in front of several hundred people. I'm too embarrassed to take her concern to the director, so we're at a standoff. Ellen and I never talk it through, and she refuses to attend the performance. I resent what seems like her petty jealousy and her absence at this high point of my co-curricular year, and some distance grows between us.

Not enough to keep us celibate, though. My continued interest in sex helps keep me from taking seriously any threats to our relationship. The fact that the sex is pleasurable should be enough to keep us together, I figure. Despite, or maybe because of the unsettledness of our marriage, we don't even think or talk about condoms, the only kind of birth control that is readily available at the time. Predictably, we learn in January that Kelsie is going to have a sister or brother a little over one year younger than her.

Having successfully coped with Kelsie's first six months—not realizing what an easy baby she is—we are fairly calm about expecting child number two. For one thing, student status and two children effectively insulate me from ever being drafted. In addition, Ellen embraces pregnancy and motherhood with enthusiasm again, and I love being loved by this incredibly darling infant girl, so I'm optimistic about having a second child. I have no sense of the long-term danger of fathering another child with someone I don't love.

Since Kelsie entered our life before Ellen and I had the opportunity to get fully settled in our own relationship, we each develop an individual connection with her. Ellen spends much more time with Kelsie than I do, which means she copes with the lion's share of dirty diapers, meltdowns, boo-boos, and baffling tears. It looks to me like Ellen responds to this imbalance with gratitude and equanimity. Motherhood not only comes naturally to her; she seems to love it and do it well.

As for me, three months into fatherhood, I begin to see how significantly my life's changing. Kelsie and school are now the two main parts of my world. Whenever I'm home and don't have a paper to write, school is at a distance, important but bracketed for now. Kelsie's radiant and infectious smile greets me enthusiastically every time I come into the room. She is delighted when I hold, jostle, and cuddle her. She smells indescribably sweet. Dad-daughter breakfasts brighten my mornings, and Mom says she appreciates the extra sleep.

I don't realize at the time how much I'm profiting from Ellen's and my developing pattern of traditional gender roles—Mom as homemaker and Dad doing his pre-professional thing while parenting evenings and some weekends. Kelsie and I unreflectively start building a typical dad-little-girl relationship, where she (rather than Ellen) is queen of my world and I'm king of hers. I start learning about genuine love the only way an immature man can—by experiencing it. Kelsie teaches me.

She loves me unconditionally, naturally, completely, and continuously and shows me how to love her the same way. She freely gives me her delighted attention and basks in mine. I tune into her life rhythms and begin offering her what I later learn to call the feeling of being felt, the sense that another valued human gets some of what it's like to live in your skin. Without awareness, reflection, guile, or the ability to articulate it, she offers me the same thing. I feel like a whole person when I'm with her. She knows, even as a toddler, how her laughter charms me, how she fills a large part of my life. I'm enchanted by her, almost literally; she has me under her spell. She responds to my awe in spontaneous, subtle, and completely candid ways, reaching, looking, smiling, nuzzling, grasping, giggling, cuddling, changing her sounds from troubled to serene. I'm utterly bedazzled.

For my junior summer, Ellen, Kelsie, and I move back into Ellen's parents' house, and Ada and my mom settle into happy grandmothering. Since bad health forced my dad to sell the grocery store, and he's now working as a janitor for the school district, he has time to spend with family, and his earlier reservations about our pregnancy disappear. He's as charmed by Kelsie as I am. Fred's around occasionally, but he mostly works and sleeps.

I'm on second shift at the cranberry and sweet corn cannery, which means I get up midmorning and drive a forklift in cold storage afternoons and evenings. We're not paying rent, and the Teamster-controlled job pays enough that I can bank funds for the school year.

In this time before cell phones, I don't learn about a frightening near-tragedy until I get home one evening. Fred and Ada's house is a boxy, two-story, steep-roofed structure with a straight upstairs run of sixteen steps behind a door right inside the front entrance. Nobody babyproofs anything these days. In fact, everybody thinks it's great that the lower cabinets in the kitchen provide Kelsie with so many pots, pans, utensils, and baking ingredients to play in and with. One downside of this freedom is that Grandma has to clean up flour and sugar messes. She hardly minds at all.

Another is that there's no barrier at the top of the stairs. Ellen informs me that Kelsie fell through the opening in the middle of this afternoon, and Ellen and Ada tell of their terror listening to sixteen loud bumps interspersed after the first three with Kelsie's scared shrieks. Happily, she was still screaming when she rolled out the stairway door. When I get home, the women are still rattled by what happened, and it appears that Kelsie's been protected from serious injury by the fact that her skull and skeleton are still mostly cartilage. I'm not only spared the worst fright, but Kelsie's especially eager to cuddle with me, which feeds my sense of myself as savior and protector.

Ellen soldiers through her second pregnancy just as she did the first time. She and I don't spend much time together, and we don't know enough about how to be a couple to worry about our parallel lives. Our sex life is diminished by my work schedule and her swollen belly, and my love life continues to revolve around Kelsie. A pattern develops this summer that will ultimately help end our marriage.

But not for a decade. Our second daughter is born one year and twenty-three days after her sister. The delivery is uneventful, and we name her Julie Ellen. It's Kelsie's turn to be fascinated and bewitched, while Ellen and I marvel at how different one daughter can be from her sister. Where Kelsie was a laid-back infant, Julie is an intense one. Kelsie eats almost anything we put in front of her, and Julie is picky. When Kelsie cries, she can be consoled, and Julie Ellen cries enough at bedtime that her grandparents pronounce her "colicky" and offer homegrown potions and advice.

Most noticeably, at least for the first few months of her life, Julie is not a beautiful baby. This is ironic, because, as a teenager and young adult, Julie's so attractive she's recruited to attend modeling school and barraged by wannabe boyfriends. Later in the girls' lives, I notice some bad blood between them around Julie's good looks. But when we make family silhouettes for gifts at Julie's first Christmas, we notice that her head is noticeably elongated, and this gives her a homely look. Of course, her mom dotes on and loves her just as Kelsie and I do. But the differences are surprising.

Two natural experts are now teaching me about love. Julie smiles, smells, cuddles, and laughs with me just like her sister. At times, the happiness that comes from being together in these ways with two young daughters almost overwhelms me. When I hold them both, joy jumps out of me, and my heart smiles. When we're together, they nudge my other life priorities into second and third place. I feel family. My head knows that Ellen's an integral part of this loving group, but in my heart, she remains on the edge of the circle.

Most of my senior year is uneventful. The debate team is on the road again a dozen weekends, and I spend large chunks of other time on campus studying, researching with my debate partner, or in student club meetings. Most days, Ellen and the girls are with their married student friends and playmates. Ellen and I agonize many nights over Julie's crying. She doesn't respond to any of the ways we've been told to cope, and we don't know whether to hold her or to let her "cry herself out." We often opt for the latter strategy even though it hurts my heart—and Ellen's—to suffer along with someone so little and defenseless. I wonder today whether some of Julie's life struggles began here.

Professor Knutson counsels me to begin my academic career by earning a master's degree and then teaching college for two years, to be sure that the profession is right for me. Only after this, he says, should I enter the several-year-long doctoral program, the completion of which is a prerequisite for any career in higher education.

So I begin the master's level graduate application process and am also encouraged by various faculty to explore Danforth, Guggenheim, and other national graduate fellowships. As part of this process, I'm gratified to learn that I'm in a close race with a classmate for valedictorian. He strikes me as a grade grubber though, and I actually don't think much about my GPA, so the news doesn't change my studying habits. At the end of our last semester, I learn that he beat me by a tenth of a point.

On the other hand, my on-campus Danforth interview reminds me that, as my sixth-grade teacher, Mrs. Gilbert, put it, "You aren't as smart as you think you are." The distinguished professor who's the Danforth representative on campus calls me into his office, and my clumsiness and lack of situational awareness lead me, without realizing it, to sit in his chair, on his side of his desk. He's gracious enough not to make a point of it, and I'm unreflective enough to stay there through the entire interview. I can't remember how poorly or well I responded to his questions, but I learn afterward that my Danforth candidacy is over.

Danforth, though, turns out to be a battle, not the war. One spring term morning, our family's awakened by a phone call from Western Union. The caller reads me a telegram from one of the nation's top schools for communication study. This university is offering me a graduate fellowship worth almost $3,000, which at this time and to us is very big money. With professor Knutson's support, I accept at the first possible moment, and Ellen and I start planning our move to the Midwest.

I'm amazed and grateful. I never dreamed that a university as prestigious as this one would give my application a second look. The program's designed to enable students to complete the master's degree in one academic year. The School of Communication includes departments of argumentation and debate, public address, speech disorders, interpretation, and radio-television-film. I'm awed by the options.

Moving eight hundred miles West is also huge for Ellen and me. Except for Ellen's brother in the army, none of our parents or siblings has ever lived in another state, and almost all our extended families have homes within a hundred miles. Nobody we know well has traveled extensively either. The trips I've taken with the debate squad have shown me places I'd never experienced, and Ellen's only seen them in the pictures I've brought home. The thought of living in a community one street away from the third largest city in the country is daunting, and we have no idea what cultural differences we'll encounter. Happily, Aunt Bette, Uncle Tom, and their daughters, Kathy and Amy, live near the school, and they are excited to be our local contact people.

My first plan is to replace our car, an idiosyncratic English Ford sedan. It's too small and too difficult to get serviced. We need a station wagon, I reason, so Kelsie and Julie can have an area behind the front seat for some toys, room to move around, and places to nap during our cross-country trip. Multibuckle safe child car seats are more than a decade away.

I unload the English Ford and find an affordable 1956 US Ford station wagon with an automatic transmission. We fit the car with a trailer hitch and load a four-by-six trailer with the belongings we have—twin beds for the girls, a cast-iron double bedstead with mattress and springs, a small kitchen table and chairs, love seat, wooden rocker, portable typewriter, chest of drawers, linens, clothes, and some kitchen utensils. We arrange the back of the station wagon for the several-day trip, padding the space with blankets, selecting the girls' favorite toys, and securing the potty chair as far away from the front seat as possible.

Our parents' financial support is limited to my dad giving us his Shell Oil credit card to cover gas and oil for the year. We say our goodbyes in early September and head West, planning our first stop at Aunt Helen and Uncle Ted's home 200 miles away. Well before we get there, it's apparent that the Ford's automatic transmission is going out. Once it's moving, the car shifts up and down okay, but each time we come to a stop, there's no telling whether it will start moving forward again. I nurse it into motion by shifting from park to neutral to drive several times, and when we roll up to Helen and Ted's, we know we'll have to have the transmission serviced. Uncle Ted finds us an honest and reasonable mechanic who tells us that he'll need to rebuild the transmission completely, so we spend three days with our generous relatives while car repairs run up a $250 bill. Dad okays putting the cost on his card, and we hit the road again.

Before we've gone fifty miles, the transmission's repeating its earlier symptoms. Ellen and I decide that our best strategy is to drive straight through, keeping stops to an absolute minimum. Kelsie and Julie seem to have picked up some of their parents' dogged determination, and they're entertaining themselves and each other, taking long naps, and even using the still-too-close potty chair.

We fill the tank and drive fifteen hours straight, making only short, engine-running stops for gas, bathroom breaks, and snacks. We collapse on the lumpy beds of a cheap motel, and the next morning, we invest two hours in letting the girls play on the motel's rickety swing set and then hit the road again. After another uncertain day, we limp into Chicago, rent a room at a sketchy hotel, and call Bette and Tom to let them know we've arrived.

The next day, Kathy and Amy happily take charge of Kelsie and Julie, Tom connects me with a friend who has tools and an empty garage for working on the car, and Ellen and Bette shop for an apartment. I locate a wrecking yard with a used transmission and torque converter that will fit the Ford, and I spend two days under the car in the borrowed garage, wrestling the 150-pound failed parts out of the Ford and the used parts back in. I'm half surprised that, when I'm done, it works. My interest in things mechanical pays off.

Ellen and Bette find an apartment in a four-story brick building in what the Realtor calls "a changing neighborhood." This means that poor black families are beginning to rent here. The building almost qualifies as a tenement, with its peeling-paint alley entrance, cockroaches, and periodically present "super." We can only afford one bedroom, but we figure that will be the girls', and we can put our bed in what's supposed to be the dining room. Plus, there's a walk-in closet that will work as my study.

The rent's $95 a month. Our budget from the fellowship is $240 a month, so we begin planning how to cover food for the four of us, car insurance, parking, whatever clothes the girls might need, and incidentals for $36 a week, plus the little backup savings we have from my summer work.

Our financial situation along with the challenge of starting a graduate degree program at a school this prestigious give me excuses to take on what I call my "graduate school affectation," smoking a pipe. I've smoked cigarettes for a couple of years, and the surgeon general has just released the first warning about their health effects. Uncle Tom responds to this announcement by quitting his pack-a-day habit cold turkey, and I decide to switch to an apparently less dangerous and clearly more distinguished-appearing practice. My inclination toward champagne tastes on a beer income, which Mom tells me I inherited from Dad, leads me to invest in two twenty-dollar pipes to supplement the fifty-cent corncobs, and I spend downtime learning about high-end tobaccos. Since nothing is known yet about secondhand smoke, Ellen and the girls accept my lighting up in the apartment and tell me that they like how it smells. I'm convinced the pipe helps me look mature and scholarly.

Maybe, you ask, but on your budget? Good point. But the "affectation" part is more important to me than the budget my habit helps break.

As you might expect, Ellen and I lose a little weight this year. Smoking a pipe helps me some. All of us get tired of Special K with skim milk breakfasts and hot dogs in baked beans for supper. But nobody goes hungry, and, thankfully, nobody needs medical care. Bette and Tom host us regularly for hearty dinners, Kathy and Amy love spending time with the girls, and Bette's connections with a nationally famous theatre company means that Ellen and I even enjoy a couple of nights out, thanks to the dress rehearsal tickets she gives us.

Thanksgiving finds us with Tom's family enjoying all the traditional dishes. Back home, friend George mails us a three-foot blue spruce so we have a live Christmas tree. Ellen and I agree to pass on presents this year, so the girls can get the dolls they want. Christmas Eve, the two of us are up past midnight to finish sewing flannel holiday nightgowns for Kelsie and Julie, and our girls spend a good part of Christmas morning opening the largesse mailed by grandparents.

Within our first two months in the apartment, the Ford's transmission fails yet again. I pour in oil thickener in an effort to get it to function long enough to sell it. The symptoms continue. I shop the local lots for a replacement set of wheels, and a salesman at the Ford & Mercury dealer pushes me toward an almost-new two-door Mercury Comet, claiming that it actually was owned by a little old lady. I tell him about the Ford's transmission history. He says he's planning on sending it to auction anyway.

When I bargain for a selling price and monthly payments that we can afford, it becomes clear that he must have paid the lady very little for her trade-in. Miraculously, we arrive at a deal. I drive the station wagon into the dealership in order to transfer belongings from it into the Comet, and after we're back home, I get a call from the dealer asking me to come and move the Ford. None of my earlier tricks work. So far as I know, it could still be there.

Unfortunately, the school's not a very good fit for me. My high school dating MO pretty well protected the male parts of my fragile ego, but I don't have a piece of armor to shield the small-town, lower-middle class parts from this school's sophistication. One day, before my History of Film class, I overhear a conversation between two undergraduates planning their weekend. They agree that it's time for a break from campus, and they settle on Saturday and Sunday in Miami. One eighteen-year-old assures the other that they can take his dad's plane. Very unlike my own undergrad experience. In this group, I'm an Other.

The next term, each student is required to give a presentation of our projects in a Radio-TV course. Mine is well researched and organized, and I'm pleased with the presentation until I discover after it's over that I've spent fifteen minutes in front of the class with my nerdy cardigan sweater buttoned crooked. Obviously a hick from the sticks.

After two terms of classes, I'm also underwhelmed by my experience as a student here. It's partly my social awkwardness and also my decision to focus my degree on radio-television-film. Unfortunately, I don't know enough, and don't have good enough advising to understand that radio-television-film is mainly a practical, hands-on enterprise. There's much to be learned, but most of it comes from doing, not studying. The literature is thin, and relatively little research has been done, which means that anyone serious about developing expertise in this area ought to be working for a film production company, one of the networks, or a local AM or FM station. By the end of the academic year, I feel as if I've spent my time, as one of my radio-TV professors actually puts it, "learning more and more about less and less."

I've done well enough academically that the department invites me to be an instructor in the Summer High School Institute, a well-established six-week session that attracts talented high school seniors from across the nation. The school's end game is obviously student recruitment, but the institute also gives participants opportunities to compete against peers who are more accomplished than their classmates back home and to take classes in topics that are co-curricular at most secondary schools. I teach argumentation and debate. I've had only one graduate class on the topic, so I'm drawing mainly on the workbook they give me and my four years' experience in debate.

This is my first opportunity to see what teaching is like. Since these are advanced placement high schoolers, the content is supposed to be first-year-university level, so it's a realistic test for me. My main challenge is figuring out how to relate to the students. I'm only a couple of years older than they are, and I'm told I look younger than that. As an undergraduate, I appreciated the international law professor who said he was going to "treat all of you as the adults you are," so I try his practices with them. I address them as "Mr." and "Ms." and close the classroom door five minutes after our start time to ensure punctuality. I let them sit where they want the first day and then make a chart of each person's place, to keep order in class and make it easier for me to learn their names.

My student evaluations at the end of the session are lousy. It's a hard lesson. The twenty young people are well behaved and timid enough not to rebel, but it's clear that they didn't like the class and didn't learn much. I should have chosen a different person to copy, one more like Prof. Knutson. In his classes, I've experienced how learning happens when people are comfortable enough with each other to engage and connect. I know that formality pushes people apart.

Christmas and the Comet are ups in this nine months of ups and downs, and our budget and the summer institute are downs. Another up happens as the four of us begin to become a family unit—a flawed one but still a family. Ellen helps make this happen.

She never complains about our impoverished situation, the time I invest in coursework, or the fact that she's the primary parent.

Each Sunday, she dresses the girls in matching outfits sent by the grandparents, we shepherd them into Sunday school classes, and afterward, she shares their excitement about what they've experienced and created. She copes with the cockroaches, ignores, for the most part, the clanking radiators, and charms the super into benefits we don't technically deserve. She builds a relationship with the older British woman across the hall, so the girls have a part-time grandma in their lives. When a woman from the leasing agency asks to use our phone and then chastises us for having a bed in the dining room, Ellen supports my writing of a snarky reply that we're not violating any part of the lease and she should mind her own business. The relationship between Ellen and me continues to be more superficial and less open than it should ideally be, but it's not because she complains, nags, or requires more attention. I probably should be learning to love her.

Instead, I continue to be charmed by Kelsie and Julie. My favorite picture from our year is of me and both girls in the rocking chair, all three of us asleep. As I write this, I can almost feel the cuddles against both sides of my body and smell the sweetness of their hair. My cheeks are a bit hollow and my arms thinner than usual, but it shows that there were times during this nine months that were genuinely happy.

CHAPTER 4

Professional Progress, Relational Strain

Sit in the front row of a movie theater, and the screen dominates your world. The overwhelming color, movement, images, and sound make it difficult to listen or look away. It's also next to impossible to reflect on what's happening, to notice, for example, how much the film fills up your awareness. You're completely caught up in what's on the screen. Crotch thinking is like this.

Marriage guru Mark Gungor makes big bucks telling audiences across the country how men get trapped in this laser focus much more often than women do.[13] Gungor claims that male brains are like a collection of hundreds of boxes, one for the car, one for the money, one for sex, one for the kids, one for the wife, and so on. The key feature of men's brains is that no one box touches any other box. They're completely separate. Women's brains, by contrast, are like big balls of wire, where everything connects with everything else. Loud laughter shows how many people in Gungor's audiences recognize themselves in his metaphor.

Crotch thinking is a kind of compartmental thinking. As Gungor reminds us, men especially can be singularly focused on one goal, one project, one deadline, one missing piece. An erection galvanizes a man's attention more completely than any work or family project, but, for example, guys are also much more able than women to ignore store displays of shirts, shoes, and swimsuits when we're shopping for underwear.

From 1964, when I complete the master's degree, through 1969, when I finish the PhD, I cycle between the professional progress box of my brain and the sex/intimacy box. As I get close to the end of my first year of graduate school, I apply for college teaching jobs that require only a master's degree. I find an opening at a small university in the upper Midwest that specializes in training nurses and industrial arts teachers. The speech department needs someone to build a debate and forensics program and teach the basic public speaking course, and I figure I can do both. The job fits my undergrad and Summer Institute experiences more than my master's work, but my disaffection with radio-television-film makes this okay. Plus, after nine months of near-poverty living in a city where we don't feel at home, we're ready to be earning a salary in a place where we can feel at home and put down tendrils, if not roots.

This department mainly provides general education classes for first- and second-year students, which means that the job would be a professional dead end for me if I stayed long-term, but it looks ideal for the two-year test that Prof. Knutson recommended.

The department chair earned his PhD where I am, so he comes here to interview whenever he has an opening, and we hit it off well. The position is instructor rank and $6,300 a year. Given our family's current budget, I figure we can put $2,000 into a savings account each year we're there. I get the offer and accept it immediately.

Before we arrive, the department chair finds us a house, "the Hosford place" he tells us, five blocks from the university. The first days we're there, we learn some of what it's like to live in a small Midwest community where I work for the town's largest employer. When we pick out a new living room set at the local furniture store, all I have to tell them to open an account is that I work at the university, and the only information they need to deliver our purchases is that we're at the Hosford place. No address required, no credit check, and no money changes hands.

My focus shifts back to work first, daughters second, and Ellen a distant third. Most of my days are filled with new course preparations, teaching, advising, and building the forensics and debate program. I spend long afternoons in the drama costume shop trying to develop the research, critical thinking, and public speaking competencies of young people who are eager and see the value of what they're trying to do but who are poorly equipped to excel in the activities that debate and forensics require. I register the school for forensics tournaments in the neighboring states and organize and launch a chapter of a national honorary. At the tournaments, my team anchors the low end of the ratings and rankings.

The two years we spend here mark the first extended time that Ellen, Kelsie, Julie, and I get to play house for real. The traditional roles Ellen and I settled into work well in this small Midwest town. Dad wins the bread, Mom makes the home, and daughters grow through their third, fourth, and fifth years. Kathy's and Amy's roles as big sisters for Kelsie and Julie are filled by my boss's two daughters. Ellen finds friends among faculty wives, and I spend the little downtime I have socializing with colleagues.

Ellen's and my sex life settles into a mundane and, for me, unsatisfying pattern. I find myself wishing we had sex more often than our common two or three times a month. But it doesn't occur to me to talk about this. I think there might be an opening for conversation when we wake up one winter morning during our first year and realize that we had sex during the night, when both of us were supposedly asleep. I initiated it, and Ellen either decided to go along or enjoyed it. We laugh nervously. Nothing else is said. Clearly a symptom.

A high point of our time here is Ellen's and my participation together in the local community theatre group. We attend meetings, participate in fundraising, and both accept roles in the group's production of *The Crucible*. Ellen has the part of Abigail Williams, the attractive leader of the young women first accused of witchcraft, and the mistress of respectable farmer John Proctor. I play Judge Danforth, who creates official opportunities for various characters to lie and thus exacerbates the worst qualities of the citizens of Salem, Massachusetts.

Five weeks of blocking, memorizing lines, and run-throughs give Ellen and me opportunities to spend enjoyable hours with each other and fellow cast members, and this is one of our best times together as a couple.

The familiarity she and I develop also begins to lead to some contempt. I'm put off by her casual approach to hygiene, for example. Since I'm faster at ironing clothes than she is, we share this task, and the smelly stains in the armpits of many of her blouses are unpleasant. I'm used to showering every day, and she isn't. Not much motivation for oral sex, if either of us were comfortable suggesting or trying it. I'm also used to changing bed linens weekly, and she isn't. I don't like the way the bed feels and smells after several weeks. I also don't know what she thinks of my pipe smoker's breath, but I can't imagine she likes it. Again, we don't talk about any of this. I just build resentments, and I suspect she does too. Our resentments surface in reduced sexual contact. And this means more unwanted erections and the frustrations that accompany them.

A year and a half pass surprisingly quickly. Ellen takes a leadership role in faculty wives, and I get to drive a fraternity's stock car in the Winter Carnival ice races. Our first December, we take the train home to spend the holidays with family. In the summer, I manage the swimming pool at the local country club. Our second year, while entering the locker room at the school's swimming pool, I catch sight of my body in a mirror. I notice that the twenty-plus pounds I've put on really show. Midwestern cheese, butter, and bratwurst cooked in beer have had their impact, especially on my belly. Like many guys in their mid-twenties, I begin to think about making healthier lifestyle choices but not very seriously.

While researching my next professional step, I discover the doctoral fellowships financed by the National Defense Education Act, one of the federal government's responses to being left behind in the space race by the Russian launch of Sputnik. The act establishes a graduate fellowship program that gives priority to students planning to be professors. NDEA fellowships cover not only tuition and fees but also stipends for graduate students to pay for books, rent, and living expenses for them and their dependents. I apply late in 1965, and early the next year, I learn that I've been awarded an NDEA fellowship by two large universities on the West Coast.

A faculty colleague and I drive West so I can visit them. I'm much more impressed with the program, students, and faculty in Los Angeles, but Ellen and I are spooked by the prospect of living a continent away from home and in the center of this big of a city, especially since the Watts riots have just happened. Nervous phone calls to UCLA's department chair elicit reassurances that the campus is a safe space and the claim that more Midwesterners live in LA than in Iowa and Wisconsin combined. My department chair also encourages me to accept the offer. So after some hesitation, Ellen and I begin planning our next move for our three-year stint in Southern California. May 1966, we pack yet another four-by-six U-Haul, hook it to the back of the Comet, and head home for the summer.

The girls are grown enough to travel pretty well, but the loaded trailer is almost too much for the Comet. It takes the better part of a mile to accelerate to freeway speed, and the heavy traffic on parts of the interstate cause the engine to overheat.

We make it back to Washburn Street, but it's clear that we should change cars again before heading West. I find a flashy white '63 Chevy hardtop with a red interior that I figure will fit right into Southern California culture.

The cannery takes me back for another summer, and the weeks pass without any more kids tumbling down Grandma and Grandpa's stairs. Ellen and the girls enjoy their time with extended family. Kelsie and Julie become permanent apples of the eyes of grandparents, aunts, uncles, and cousins. The fact that we're not paying rent means once again that I can build our savings account with my forklift-driving wages. Ellen and I spend more time at work (me) and with the girls (both of us) than with each other. Late August, we pay for the familiar U-Haul rental and pack the trailer for our three thousand mile trek west—the eighth move in our four-year marriage.

The Chevy handles the trailer easily, and we make the trip to LA without problems. As we move in, we immediately notice striking differences between this university living experience and our others during my B.A. and M.A. programs. We're assigned a two-bedroom, ground-floor unit in one of the university's almost-new married student high-rises. Our apartment includes a decent-sized kitchen with dining area, living room that opens onto a private patio, well-appointed bath upstairs, master bedroom large enough for a king-sized bed (although we don't have one), second bedroom for the girls, and ample closet space. The three married student buildings on a corner of UCLA's campus enclose a well-kept courtyard, providing a large play area with sandboxes, grassy spaces, and almost-new play equipment. To us, it's luxurious. Clearly, UCLA doesn't do tacky. And the fellowship pays our rent.

Kelsie's five, and Julie's four, so we search for a preschool. Following the advice of some new neighbors, we talk to the principal of a private elementary school about fifteen minutes from campus. Their preschool starts at age four, and we're impressed by their administration, faculty, and high standards. The school's principal tells us that their graduates commonly score one or two grades above their level when they enter high school. Ellen and I agree that we want to give the girls this kind of opportunity and challenge in their early schooling.

I'm still surprised when both girls show up with homework each afternoon. Kelsie is expected to spend an hour on her assignments, and Julie half an hour. This is at age five and four! But both girls love their teachers and the school, and tuition will almost be covered by my summer cannery wages. I encourage Ellen to find a job to help the budget.

Campus employment is eager to support graduate student families, so Ellen interviews for a position in the Dental School. She's hired almost immediately, and the job is ideal. Ellen works on campus, can adjust her hours to fit the girls' schedules, and is happy to be mentored by Rosa, a senior administrator who immigrated years earlier from Guadalajara. This placement and Rosa's strong support make Ellen curious about longer-term possibilities in the dental field. I'm delighted by her positive thoughts about a professional career. Not only would her salary boost our income, but we both would be on promising professional employment trajectories. And now that I see what's likely ahead for me, I'd prefer to be married to a career woman rather than a stay-at-home mom.

I'm one of eleven NDEA fellows beginning UCLA's PhD program in the communication department. With the department's encouragement, the group begins regular study sessions, social events, and other collaborations that define a cohort. I spend increasing amounts of time with the group, leaving Ellen and the girls to make their own friends.

In the LA Basin, UCLA has a reputation as a business-friendly, professionally focused school. So when a city prosecuting attorney is trying a pornography case involving a stack of pulp paperbacks, and he's concerned that the jury will read only the juicy passages if he simply gives them copies of the books, he calls the chair of the communication department to hire some graduate students to read the books aloud in court. All the titles need to be read, cover to cover, to meet the part of the Supreme Court's current definition of pornography as, "the work, taken as a whole, appeals to prurient interests."

A classmate named Frank and I get the job, which pays each of us forty dollars an hour, more than double any hourly wage I've ever earned. After slogging through only a few of what turn out to be boring rather than titillating books, the attorneys work out a settlement, and the gig ends. But not before fattening our bank accounts.

A ride back to campus with Frank and the attorney underscores how much I don't fit into this new culture any better than I fit into my M.A. school. I'm dressed in my best Hart, Schaffner, and Marx suit that I bought to interview for my first job, and driving the three-year-old Chevy. On the way, the attorney tells me that he bought a suit just like mine "several years ago" and that he "gave it to Goodwill" last Thanksgiving. Subtle.

A few minutes later, we pull up to the campus gate, and I begin to respond candidly to the guard's questions—that we want to drive through campus to show our passenger where the department is. The attorney immediately figures out that drive-throughs are disallowed, so he interrupts me to spin a tale about our "actual" intent, and the guard waves us through. Nobody says anything, but it's obvious who's the bumpkin. *This needs to change*, I think to myself.

It starts to change when, after a year at the oral surgery job, Ellen finds a position with more clinical contact working in the one-man office of a middle-aged general practice dentist. With the cooperation of some of his patients, Dr. Sawyer is engaged in an informal professional development program focused on orthodontia. So although he's not certified, he offers teeth-straightening services at a relatively low cost to help him learn how to do it. Ellen's position comes with the benefit of free dental care for the family. So Dr. Sawyer takes impressions, builds me a retainer, and grinds off the excess length of my top incisors. After several months of wearing the retainer, my smile begins to resemble the Southern California norm. No more buckteeth.

In the middle of my second year, the chair gets another call for consulting services, this time from an architecture and engineering firm headquartered in Pasadena. The firm has the contract for the design, construction management, and interior finishing of a worldwide hotel chain. They are interested in communication training for their project managers, and three of us from the cohort take on the project. We design a four-week program that meets two evenings a week and price our services at fifty dollars an hour for preparation and delivery time. We decide not to charge for our commute. This means our fee will be $3,600 for the program, $1,200 apiece. At the time, a new Ford Mustang costs about $2,000.

The firm accepts our proposal, including the fee, without question or complaint, which from my point of view is astounding. The training goes well, and this experience gives me a taste for communication consulting work, a challenging and lucrative sideline that I pursue for over thirty years. In graduate school, and especially after, this work helps fund my forays into upscale cars, boats, and fashionable clothes.

Frank and I also get a gig serving champagne at an exclusive party in the Hollywood Hills. We're required to show up in white dinner jackets and are briefed on how to behave, open bottles, and pour. Both of us get handy at charming attractive and fashionably clad young women by shooting champagne corks off a balcony that overlooks palm trees, bougainvillea, winding roads, and the red tile roofs of Spanish style mansions. Another fifty-dollar-an-hour job.

These experiences and the higher income expectations associated with the fellowship, my side earnings, and Ellen's job speed my immersion into Southern California culture. It's new to both Ellen and me and different from what we're used to. I lap it up much more than she does.

Where I grew up in the Northeast, so many days are gray that when the sun shows itself, most people make any excuse they can to get outside, if possible to the water. In LA, the sun shines all the time, which means you don't even have to plan when to go to the beach. New Year's Day? Head for the Santa Monica Pier; you can count on it being warm enough to swim.

Another difference is that families in smaller towns of the Northeast and Midwest generally practice sincerity and humility; in Southern California, it's all about flash and dazzle. Your car should be new or nearly new, clean and well waxed, and at least a little tricked out. Foreign is ideal, and the more expensive, the better. Most people have access to a private or nearly private pool, and although only deadbeats and losers spend all day in the plastic deck chairs, it's a great place to work on your tan and to be seen.

People also pay more attention to every part of personal appearance. There are more straight white teeth in the LA Basin than anywhere else on earth. Women from twelve to forty display long, preferably blonde hair, and men of the same ages trust their stylists—nobody relies on a barber—to coif their locks in ways that echo the current Hollywood A-listers. Shorts, sundresses, and muscle shirts expose a maximum of skin for sexual display and encourage both bodybuilding and relaxed expectations about intimate contact. Women pay close attention to their breasts, waists, and legs, often with the help of their plastic surgeons, and men try to harden their abs and build definition in their biceps and pecs. Plus, everybody has at least a couple of cocktails every evening, and nobody prefers inexpensive beer or wine.

Sound exaggerated? As you know, graduate students are notoriously impoverished. Masters and doctoral students inhabit the culture of Top Ramen and Chef Boyardee, of small wardrobes replenished in thrift stores, of box wine and Busch light. Yet, during the three years and a summer that it took me to complete the PhD, evidence of how deeply I drank the Southern California Kool-Aid includes the following:

- Eighteen months into the program, I replace the Chevy with my first Mercedes, a three-year-old 220S sedan.
- Kelsie and Julie attend private school all three years.
- My wardrobe expands to include, among other things, an ice-cream striped sport coat and my first four custom-made shirts with Hollywood-high, long-point collars and french cuffs—twenty-five dollars apiece.
- I discover private plane travel when a neighbor teaching ROTC and working on his commercial and instrument

- ratings invites me to join him for several evenings of touch-and-goes at an airport near the ocean, and on weekend trips to San Diego-Tijuana and Las Vegas.
- My consulting practice expands during my third year when I'm hired by a Big Eight accounting firm to provide communication training for all their new employees. My hourly rate goes up again, and I enjoy perks like an expense account and first-class air travel.
- After two years in married student housing, we spend year three renting the comfy home of a San Pedro faculty member on sabbatical, hosting both sets of parents and other family members, and enjoying avocados, oranges, and lemons from trees in our backyard.
- I find a hairstylist who encourages me to get used to a more Hollywood-length cut without any part. I draw the line at her desire to add color, but my look changes significantly.
- Our trips to Disneyland and SeaWorld happen so frequently that the girls become blasé about the attractions.

By the start of my third year in the program, I've finished the required coursework and have approval from my supervisory committee to proceed with the dissertation. A large share of my time this semester is also dedicated to job shopping. The University of Arizona invites me to Tucson for an interview, and I work on imagining what it would be like to live in the high desert.

Then, after midterm, a position opens at UMass, the institution I avoided as an undergraduate. At that time, I was afraid of the place because of its size. As an almost newly minted PhD, I'm attracted by the opportunity to join a big-league school—one that offers the doctorate—and to return to the part of the country that's home.

I sweat over my application materials and get input from my doctoral supervisor and other professors. I get invited for an interview, part of which is a presentation that, I learn later, strikes one of the senior professors as "brash." Despite his reservations, I get the offer for fall, 1969: instructor rank (assistant professor as soon as I complete the PhD) and $10,500 a year. Tucson is forgotten. Especially because I know I can supplement my income with consulting wages in and around Amherst, I again accept as soon as I can.

Dissertation writing, like much of the rest of the PhD, is an endurance contest more than a test of intellect. First you write a prospectus that has to pass muster with each member of your supervisory committee. It takes several months to jump through the hoops held up by each of the three.

After the prospectus is approved, you have to be willing to spend long hours doing research, which in pre-computer 1969 means time in the library, tracking down obscure books and articles in professional journals only read by a handful of the scholars in the fields the journals serve.

I'm absent and distracted enough by all this that Ellen decides, at the end of Kelsie and Julie's school term, to head to her parents' and leave me alone for the summer to finish the dissertation. This decision is a comment on the state of our relationship, and I don't notice that it is—which is another comment on the state of our relationship.

Part of what makes it easier for her to take the girls and leave is that she sees how I've adopted many of the values of LA culture, including the importance of what I drive, how I dress and look, where to eat out, the desirability of smoking exotic pipe tobacco, and, most consequentially, how my wife looks and how she reflects on me. Ellen's short stature, grooming patterns, and small-town, blue-collar values guarantee that she sometimes appears, well, dumpy. Not stylish. Not flashy. Not always professional. Lower-middle class. The LA experiences I've had have changed me—my housing, appearance, clothing, leisure activity, and now my relationship preferences.

Apparently oblivious to all this—since we never talk about it, who's to say for sure—we agree that she and the girls should head East while I finish. We pack up what we want to keep and ship it to her folks, and the three of them leave me in June to tough out the final stages of the dissertation process. My base of operations is another house-sitting arrangement, this time at a bungalow in Thousand Oaks owned by a cohort colleague on a summer-long vacation with his family.

So here I am: alone for over two months in a three-bedroom house in an LA suburb with a 250-page writing project to complete. My typewriter, reams of paper, and stacks of books and articles occupy most of the dining room. I have a food supply consisting mainly of frozen dinners, frozen entrees, frozen pizza, and cheap wine. My calendar includes only weekly appointments with my adviser to check my progress and give me feedback on what I wrote the previous week.

Next door are a group of single male and female twentysomethings who enjoy partying evenings and weekends and who are eager for me to join them. I'm three thousand miles away from my wife and family. I'm coming off at least a year of a steadily deteriorating relationship with Ellen, due mainly to my getting sucked more and more into SoCal culture while she focuses on being a working mom.

Erections, many of them unwanted, are a frequent part of my experience. LA smog makes running outside unhealthy, and I don't have access to a pool, so I can't easily use intense physical activity to deal with my sexual frustration. I don't find the single woman next door particularly attractive, but, as misogynists say, "All cats look gray in the dark," right?

One Friday night, four of us, including her, are in a karaoke bar rocking out to Tina Turner's "Proud Mary," and the song, the drinks, and the dancing loosen me up considerably. She and I dance together, and she looks better to me than she has before. She's hesitant, but we end up at my place together and progress rapidly from necking to heavy petting on the couch. She gifts me with my first experience of fellatio, and only my semi-drunken state keeps me from coming before she's had her own enjoyment. When we're both finished, we sleep for a couple of hours. She makes her way back home early in the morning. Over breakfast, as I think about what's happened, it's easier than it probably should be for me to attribute the sex to alcohol and separation from Ellen. Lots of guys use a woman's mouth to masturbate, I tell myself. No reason to make anything out of it.

Fortunately, I only have a few more weeks of this matrimonially precarious existence to avoid my neighbor. It helps that she also appears to think of it as a one-night stand.

I deliver a complete draft of the dissertation to the committee, and ten days later, my adviser tells me they've agreed to schedule an oral defense. This is the next-to-last big hurdle in the degree program. Ellen and the girls are happy to hear it's scheduled.

On the appointed day, I drive to campus and respond to the three professors' questions for an hour and a half. The committee agrees that the degree will be granted at the next possible time in UCLA's academic calendar, January 1970.

My adviser throws a party for me at his home, and I celebrate with most of the cohort members, departmental faculty, and families. I have more than a little to drink again, and to this day, I don't remember driving the forty minutes on the freeway from my adviser's home in Pomona to the place in Thousand Oaks. Had I been stopped, I'm sure I would have blown over the legal limit.

It takes me a week to make the required changes in the manuscript, and after my adviser approves them, I hand the document to a guy known across campus as a dissertation facilitator. He walks the document around to get signatures, shepherds its progress through the library office that checks bibliography and footnote form, and expedites its getting microfilmed and bound.

My tenth high school reunion happens in a few days. I visit my hairstylist, load my clothes and writing supplies in the Mercedes, and hit the road East. I push hard for three and a half very long days, and make the reunion just after it's started. My straightened teeth, styled hair, long-pointed collar, and money clip produce their desired effect. Kelly especially notices my new look. No more "Kiss me, buckteeth!"

CHAPTER 5

Temptation Rules Again

A bomb with the force of a case of dynamite explodes in the foyer of the ROTC building on June 29, 1969, just a few weeks before I start work at the university. In early August, police and students battle each other in the University District, and a few months after I begin teaching, the Fire Department extinguishes an arson fire in the building that houses my department and the department of political science. My office is in a small WWII-vintage temporary frame structure a few steps behind this building.

Everybody notices the violence, of course. I smell the smoke as I'm evacuating with my class. Several of my students say they were part of the group who blocked the main interstate to protest the US invasion of Cambodia. But even though students and faculty across campus are demonstrating, and my office is in a highly flammable structure with no sprinklers or fire extinguishers, I remain almost completely disconnected from the political and social justice activities raging around me.

I've seen the famous radical political science professor in the building, but I have no idea what his organization, the People's Liberation Front, is about or why he's been arrested. I'd have a difficult time quickly finding Cambodia on a world map, and although I've followed television news reports of the student deaths at Kent State, they seem far away. Such is my narrow focus on my own professional and personal concerns.

Early on, I have to pay attention to family. Our house search is made easier by the help of a colleague who graduated from the same Presbyterian school I attended as an undergraduate. He and his family live in a new development north of the university. Given the tastes I've developed in Southern California, none of the older homes we look at near the campus impresses me much, and, as in most cities, you can get new construction and more house for your money by buying out of town. So we select a nearly finished trilevel with a bonus room in the development where my colleague's family lives. It's a straight shot down the interstate to the corner of campus. Thirty minutes when the traffic is light. Later, I learn it can be more than an hour when it's not.

The Dow is at 800, gas is $0.35 a gallon, and the average cost of a home here is $17,550. We pay $26,250 and get a loan from Ellen's uncle Gene to cover the down payment. My take-home pay is just over $900 a month, which makes our $308 monthly house payment (plus $55 to Uncle Gene) close to a budget buster. But, we figure, we've been in worse financial shape. My salary is bound to improve; I should be able to do some consulting; Ellen can get a job; and at least we're living in a place with some flash and dazzle.

My main responsibility is to direct a recently created, multi-section course taught by several graduate students I am expected to train and supervise. The content is new to them and to me. I've never taught this material, and I had only one related class in my doctoral program, so I'm on a crash course to learn about this part of the field. Colleagues make it clear to me that I am also expected to publish (or perish), which means I have to move rapidly to turn my dissertation into an article ready for submission to a national journal. I am quickly learning what it means to engage productively in the three responsibilities of a university faculty member: research, teaching, and service.

I'm also stumbling through the process of defining and owning my new identity in the classroom. Several older colleagues insist on being called "doctor" or "professor," only consulting with students during office hours and filling class time with monologues delivered from behind lecterns. Steve, a colleague near my age, is known among students for his dramatic and engaging lectures, occasionally given in a costume appropriate to the topic and from atop a table or desk.

Despite my experience in the Summer Institute, I wear a tie and sport coat each day of first term, carry my fat leather briefcase into each class, and keep the movable desks in neat rows. I learn again that these practices are inconsistent with the informal communication content I'm teaching, though, and my student evaluations are laced with complaints about my inaccessibility and unnecessary formality. So without fully realizing where it might lead—sound familiar?—I shift professional identities.

Second term finds me tieless, leaving the briefcase in my office, and arranging desks in a U shape or rough circle. Sometimes I stake out a seat on the chalkboard side of the room or at the open end of the U, and in some classes, I purposefully sit in different spots each day. I spend time before class in small talk with students and encourage them to drop by my office to chat. When I get moved out into the main building, I dedicate a Sunday afternoon to painting my new office light blue with dark blue super-graphics. I construct a wooden insert for my large office window that provides eight shelves for small plants and arrange my space so there's no desk between me and the person coming through the door. My boss, the department chair, can't figure out what made me think it was okay for me to paint the space, especially the way I did. Better to ask for forgiveness than permission, I figure.

These moves are greeted with grudging admiration from younger colleagues and silent skepticism from senior professors. Some in both groups are worried about having a "touchy-feely" colleague. My student ratings improve dramatically, though, and I like the increasing fit between what I'm teaching and who I'm being.

CROTCH THINKING

Students call me by my first name, and I work to learn each of their first names by the end of the first week of the term—not an easy goal in a class of fifty or sixty. I spend longer hours on campus; some of the time, students whom I've gotten to know bring in hot sandwiches for dinner from an upscale shop in the District. I dress increasingly informally, though never in jeans. I'm making faculty and student friends.

One of these is a first-year undergraduate named Judy whose intelligence and engagement earn the top grade in my basic interpersonal course. Her professional goal is to be an attorney. She's about to undergo orthopedic surgery to correct severe scoliosis, and she and her parents have arranged for her to spend her six months of body-cast recovery in the university's Student Health Center. The main requirement for this arrangement is that she continues full-time student registration in independent studies with various professors. Steve and I both agree to work with her. I draft a reading list of books and articles that are primary sources in the philosophy, theory, and psychology of communication, and we agree on several writing assignments.

Judy's surgery involves straightening the s-curve of her spine, fusing almost all the vertebrae in her back to keep her spine straight, and inserting stainless rods to hold the fix in place. One outcome of the surgery is that Judy gains almost three inches of height. The six-month recovery period gives her the opportunity to grow her hair long and keep it straight, in the style of Joni Mitchell and Cher. A downside is that she's prescribed ample pain meds by the nurturing doctor who runs the health center. I don't notice at the time, but this doctor's generosity helps trigger a pattern in Judy that will ultimately be life-destroying.

After Judy recovers enough to have visitors, Steve and I individually spend long hours with her, sitting at her bedside as we discuss the readings, helping arrange her space so she can type the required papers, and passing time in small talk. For me, this begins another hugely consequential relationship that I naively believe is benign.

At home, Kelsie and Julie are adjusting well to their new teachers and classmates. Predictably, their private schooling gives them a leg up in most of their public school classes. They find friends who live only blocks away and get involved in school activities. Both appreciate having their own room. Kelsie, who's brunette, wants a lavender and white color scheme, and Julie, who's blonde, prefers everything yellow.

I'm bringing home, especially to my relationship with Ellen, expectations and values influenced by my LA and large university experiences. A main one is that I want to be married to a career woman. We could use the money to add sparkle to our lifestyle, I reason, and I see myself as a young, decent-looking, upwardly mobile professional who can best be complemented by a wife with similar qualities. It seems natural for me to treat Ellen as a "type of wife" because, although I don't know it at the time, in the twelve years we've been together, I've never figured out what it means to recognize the uniqueness of a spouse and to unconditionally accept who she is because I love her.

I do love Kelsie and Julie. My parenting is framed by my complete acceptance of each of them, just as they are. While I want to help them grow into healthy, happy, productive, and responsible people, I have no agenda to change their developing identity. Julie's independence, willingness to take risks, and ever-present energy make her a fairly high-maintenance child, and although I want her to learn discipline and boundaries, I wouldn't change her for the world. Kelsie is less assertive than I think she ought to be, and I want to encourage her to stand up for her own beliefs. But she's also intelligent, kind, caring, and empathic, and, again, I love her just as she is. When either daughter misbehaves, I view her as having made an error, not as being an incomplete or flawed person. I'd step in front of a bullet or a speeding truck for either of them.

But I'd like Ellen to change. She originally got pregnant because, to put it this way, she might have been in love with me, or just in love with being in love, but I was in love with sex, not with the unique person she is. I didn't know then that she would prefer to be a homemaker. I didn't know that she doesn't find a lot to like about academic life, so she's not excited about engaging my world or entering a degree or professional certificate program.

Now it's clear that her preference isn't good enough for me. I think she's failing to develop her full potential and being lazy. When I put what I view as these shortcomings together with my lingering dissatisfaction about her hygiene and blue-collar values, my resentments build. Like most conflicts about identity, these are impossible for us to work through on our own. And they do nothing for our sex life.

This becomes especially obvious in winter break of my second year at. Ellen reconnects with Rosa, her supervisor and mentor at UCLA's Dental School, and Rosa invites us to visit her in Guadalajara. We schedule the trip for the break week and arrange for a graduate student couple from the department to stay with the girls.

Rosa meets us at the airport and gives us a tour of Guadalajara. She shares with us several of her favorite places and events, including the displays of fiery-colored mosaics and pottery in Tlaquepaque and the mariachi music at various outdoor restaurants. Then Rosa buys us three seats on a second-class bus to Puerto Vallarta, her favorite vacation spot on the Sea of Cortez.

The bus ride is terrifying. The narrow, mountainous road curves sharply around headlands, dips into valleys, and climbs steep hills. Some outside curves lack even rudimentary guardrails, and more than once I resort to scrunched eyes and fervent prayer. Our driver seems unaware of the cars, small and large trucks, and other busses that crowd our rear bumper, belch smoke from just in front of us, and pass us on hills and bridges. It's a relief to arrive at the Rosita Hotel, near the north end of the town.

The Rosita's located so that its pool is literally on the sand, and we enjoy spending time in the surf and drying off under a convenient *palapa* while vendors stroll by selling locally made trinkets or chanting, "*Naranjas, naranjas.*"

Our room is furnished with three beds. Ellen and I have the one closest to the window, the one in the middle is a spot for stray clothes, and Rosa sleeps in the one closest to the door. We spend all our shopping, walking, sunbathing, and sightseeing time together.

The third day, Rosa makes it clear that she is going out by herself and indicates that she means this as an opportunity for Ellen and me to spend the afternoon together making love. The two of us don't get it until she's been gone over an hour. She has expectations about what young married couples do that don't fit us. We haven't had sex for several weeks, and neither of us is thinking of this tropical paradise as a place for romance. A very clear symptom.

By contrast, back at home, Julie, Kelsie, and I have some super times. They're still girls rather than young women, which means Daddy still gets treated as special. We have fun at breakfast, when I use Hershey's syrup to make chocolate Cream of Wheat and pour juice and milk from containers I hold three feet above the table. Without spilling a drop, usually. I also decide that each deserves a special bedroom, and since we can't afford to hire a decorator or contractor, I decide to do it myself.

Kelsie wants a four-poster bed with canopy, plus matching dresser, desk, and shelves. I find an unfinished furniture shop that offers inexpensive versions of the bed and shelves, and locate a desk and dresser that only need repainting. Ellen shops for the bedspread, dust ruffle, pillow shams, canopy cover, and chair pads. Sanding, painting, and assembling take a couple of weekends, and the fumes from gallons of lavender and quarts of white paint test all of us. Kelsie loves the results.

Julie and I decide that a wall of bright yellow cabinets with a window seat would be perfect in her room. I have no woodworking experience, but a neighbor has a table saw, router, and other tools I can borrow, and plywood's relatively easy to work with. Before I'm finished, I know firsthand why custom cabinets are so expensive. My scrap pile requires an extra trip to the dump. But the bright yellow paint masks most of my mistakes, and Julie is delighted. I love helping create these spaces for them, and I think they love the fact that I did it. I continue to bask in their attention and approval.

After some months, Ellen grudgingly agrees to apply for the dental hygiene program at one of the nearby community colleges. She learns that recent changes in the law permit hygienists to perform "expanded duties," which include giving injections and condensing and carving fillings. I'm pleased with the increased status this brings to the profession, and Ellen is less pleased because she has to cope with more difficult course and skill requirements.

This is another example of the inequity in our identity change expectations. My move from student to professor status naturally comes with changes in how I see myself and how I want others to see me. Some version of the same shift will likely happen when Ellen becomes a dental hygienist. But at this point, her idea of a move toward maturity is for us to be playing bridge with several couples in the neighborhood and getting a picnic table so we can invite neighbors to grill out. I want us to move in the direction our Mercedes encourages. Symphony concerts. Skiing lessons. Maybe constructing our own wine cellar in a corner of the garage.

Historically, we wouldn't talk about any of this. Now, though, probably because we're both feeling more committed to our preferences and aware of our disconnections, we get into arguments that surface shorthand or superficial elements of this disagreement over identities.

I argue that the monthly budget will benefit from the added income she'll bring home when I'm actually thinking more of how we'll look to others when we have the accouterments the money will enable us to buy. She complains about me nagging her into returning to school, because I should know that she's always wanted to stay at home. She's also noticing the longer hours I'm spending at work and taking away from family. I'm concerned enough to suggest that we get some marriage counseling. Ellen refuses. She's never been to a counselor before, doesn't want to air our dirty laundry to anyone else, and thinks we can work it out on our own.

We maintain appearances pretty well by showing up for bridge sessions and occasionally attending university-related functions. In December of my third year in the department, we get an invitation to a Christmas party from my ex-student Judy, who's now in her senior year. Steve is her Interdisciplinary Studies adviser; she has recently been inducted into Phi Beta Kappa; and she is still planning to attend law school. Judy and two roommates have an apartment a few blocks off campus, which means a half-hour drive for Ellen and me to and from the party. The gathering includes colleagues and their spouses, plus past and present students and their dates.

I definitely notice how much Judy's changed from when she took my class and when Steve and I worked with her at the health center. I've always appreciated her intelligence, analytic abilities, and writing skills. But now, she's also strikingly attractive and much more mature. Before, she was short, plump, and average looking. Now she's taller and much slenderer, with straight brunette hair down to the middle of her back. A beautiful and desirable young woman.

At the end of the evening, she and one of her roommates are standing near the door saying goodbye and thanking people for coming. I don't remember how she's interacting with others, but I give her what I think is an appropriately brief hug, and she kisses me on the mouth. I don't mean to be corny, but I almost stumble from the impact, and my crotch responds so strongly that I'm afraid Ellen notices. I don't remember us talking much on the drive home.

The Christmas and New Year holidays pass pretty normally, and, because of the growing distance between Ellen and me, they're not quite the family celebrations they've been in the past. Kelsie and Julie, who are eleven and ten, are excited about their new bicycles and other gifts. I spend most of my time in my home office working on a textbook that a major publisher has recently asked me to assemble and edit. It's designed for the new course I've been teaching, and the publisher plans to market the book to all the schools nationwide that offer this course. The rest of my down time, I'm thinking with my crotch, fantasizing about Judy's kiss and what it might mean.

Consistent with my dating MO from high school, I hesitate contacting Judy. It's easier for her to find a reason to come by my office early the next term, though, and, as we talk, we both notice that our relationship's changed. We pay a different kind of attention to each other. We talk about different topics—her fears about having to retake the Law School Application Test, my interest in where she plans to attend law school, a little bit about my dissatisfaction at home. I don't think I'm making up what that kiss meant.

Our conversations become more frequent and longer, first over coffee on campus and then extending over lunch at student haunts near the university. Since her apartment is close, I make that an excuse for me to walk her home from a couple of these lunches, and then to come inside to talk. The first time I kiss her goodbye, it's curtains for both of us. We know exactly where we're heading, and, in what is a familiar pattern for me, we don't talk about it.

At home, Ellen is in the first difficult year of the dental hygiene program. Head and Neck Anatomy is one of her most challenging classes; in another, she's required to carve each individual tooth out of a chunk of soap. It becomes more challenging for her to balance school and family and to have any time for a social life that might include me. We drift further apart.

One February afternoon, I'm pushing Judy to progress around the bases on her living room couch, and one of her roommates unexpectedly returns home. The two of us bounce away from each other in a guilty and fruitless attempt to look like we're just conversing. College roommates, of course, have understandings about such situations, and Diane greets me brightly and heads to her room "to study." I gather that I probably look to her like an interesting catch, married or not, and she doesn't want to rain on Judy's parade.

The fourth or fifth time we're together at Judy's apartment, we're engaged in what, at the time, can only be called making out. She notices the bulge in my crotch and tells me that her roommates won't be home for hours. I ask her about birth control, and she says that she's inserted her diaphragm. The idea that she'd hope we would have sex is a dramatic turn-on for me. We tear at other's clothes like teenagers and embrace passionately. I'm as excited and almost as mindless as I was the first time with Ellen.

Judy's obviously not a virgin, and her beauty and youthful enthusiasm deliciously contrast with how Ellen and I are in bed together now. Judy's breasts aren't like Ellen's full bust, but her firm nipples suggest that she's enjoying us as much as I am. When her long hair brushes over my chest, it's like living a fantasy. I feel attractive, valued, lusted after. I realize on the way home, and this is the extent of my reflection at the time, that Judy and I have created a before and after in our relationship and that it's impossible to unring this exciting bell.

A few weeks later, Judy tells me she's moved to a new apartment several miles from campus. Now we don't have to cope with roommates, but the new location forces us to plan our liaisons more deliberately and to create and check excuses with each other. Our passion for being together makes us more than willing to undergo the inconvenience. We find ways to have sex at least twice a week, each for as many orgasms as possible.

As the retake of the LSAT gets closer, Judy gets increasingly laser focused. One afternoon, I come by to encourage her, and I'm surprised to find empty quart bottles of Tab, a then-popular diet version of Coca-Cola, on just about every flat surface of her apartment. Judy is a little uncomfortable as I count fifty-five of the dead soldiers. She tells me they've accumulated over several days. I tease her a little—backing off when she gets embarrassed. Years later, I realize that the bottles were a clear sign that I missed completely.

Alan is another student I've begun working closely with, and at first it doesn't occur to me that he'll connect with Judy. Alan is in his fifties and completing the coursework for a PhD in an interdisciplinary program that links literature, philosophy, and communication. My philosophy minor at UCLA and my current work in communication fit his project well. We also develop a friendship, and he invites me on a Saturday sailing trip in Boston Harbor. I like both Alan and the prestige value of sailing, and I'm fascinated by the knowledge and skills that sailing requires, so with Alan's encouragement, I become an eager and regular crew member. Since Ellen doesn't express any interest in my new enthusiasm, I build my own sailing relationships with Alan, his teaching and sailing partner, Frances, and their spouses, Mary and Sam.

In spring term, Judy is excited to learn that she's been accepted at a Midwest law school. We acknowledge the separation that her professional preparation will require and continue seeing each other as frequently and secretly as we can.

After Judy's graduation, which I strategically avoid, Alan and Frances invite me to spend two days helping bring the sailboat back from a cruise, and I eagerly accept. Without telling Ellen, I ask Judy to give me a ride to the small harbor town where I'll meet the boat. On the way, we're waiting for a ferry crossing, and both get the juvenile and delightful idea that we ought to take advantage of a remote meadow atop a hill overlooking the water.

As everyone knows who's done it, sex outside is risky. There's the danger of being discovered, the threats of uncomfortable rocks and sharp sticks, wind blowing underwear away, and the absence of a place to freshen up afterward. We agree that the risks are worth it.

When Judy and I arrive at the boat, it's obvious to Alan and Frances that we're together, and even though they know I'm married and have children, they accept us without judgment. It's the first time Judy and I are "out" as a couple, and we enjoy it. We spend the night on a makeshift bunk in the cockpit of the twenty-nine-foot sloop, Judy returns to town the next morning, and I set off with Alan and Frances.

The three of us on the boat can't help but talk about my relationship with Judy. A new feature of this particular instance of thinking with my crotch is that I'm in some ways actually reflecting about what I'm doing. I'm pretty distanced from Ellen, but I'm worrying about Kelsie and Julie and feeling guilty about how my involvement with Judy will affect them. Since I still see myself as serially monogamous, I'm assuming Ellen and I will divorce, and I'm afraid of how split custody and my absence will affect the girls.

Alan and Frances bring to the table the current cultural belief that children of divorce are resilient. If estranged parents don't badmouth each other, so the story goes, and if there can be collaboration around property and custody decisions, most divorces are little more than speed bumps in the participants' lives. In response to the dramatically rising rate of failed marriages, some popularized research even suggests that divorce doesn't usually do long-term damage to anyone. Alan also says he's noticed that I'm not happy about my home situation and that he wasn't surprised when I showed up with another woman. The two of them agree that the time apart while Judy is in law school will be a good test of our relationship, and they are generally supportive.

They're right that Judy's departure late in the summer leaves me seriously uncomfortable. My pattern of "going deep" in relationships hasn't changed, and I spend hours typing long love letters, listening to her favorite music, and fantasizing. Many afternoons, I sprawl on the living room floor playing LPs by Cat Stevens, Judy's—and now my—favorite performer. I try to maintain my normal relationship with the girls, and I recognize that Ellen is probably noticing how much I've moved away from her. We're still under the same roof and yet not really together.

After consulting with our department chair, a colleague and I sign a textbook contract with a national publisher headquartered in California for what is for me a second book. The publisher wants us to attend their sales meeting to explain our new book to the sales force, so they can take full advantage of the expanding market.

CROTCH THINKING

I'm missing Judy enough that I work out another example of thinking with my crotch. I decide that, since our flight will pass over Judy's school, there's no reason I can't stop off and see her on the way back. So I modify the ticket from the publisher and let her know when I'll arrive. I figure there's no reason to tell my colleague until after our presentation and after we enjoy the publisher's hospitality. I'm amazed that he isn't more surprised than he is when I tell him we won't be flying home together. Looks like what's going on is obvious to many people in the department.

Judy is one of the first cohort of women who have been admitted to this law school, and she's been assigned housing in what was, until recently, an undergraduate dorm. Since it would be awkward for her to host a visitor, she reserves a room in the on-campus hotel, and we spend most of the short time I'm there in bed together.

Judy's experiencing considerable residual pain from her surgery. Her orthopedist believes that she may need another operation to remove the stainless rods on either side of her spine. This might be an opportunity, she tells me, to transfer to Law School in Springfield, only twenty-five miles away, for her last two years. At this point, though, she's not optimistic. I get a brief tour of campus and have plenty of time on the return flight to fantasize about being with Judy. Crotch thinking overrides my concerns about how resilient Kelsie and Julie are actually going to be.

In these ways, the train keeps moving down the track. Ellen and I make plans together for the girls' eleventh- and twelfth-year Christmases. I'm much more excited, though, about finding a sterling silver craftsman who agrees to sculpt a silver seagull mounted on a small piece of driftwood as my gift for Judy. I insist on paying cash, because I don't want there to be any canceled check or credit card receipt to create a paper trail. What a tangled web we weave …

Judy mobilizes a letter from her orthopedist and a surgery appointment in early January to persuade the law school admission office to admit her, so I get to give her the silver seagull in person. We agree that I'll wait to visit her until she's moved from the hospital to the university health center for recovery. She's released just in time to begin winter term classes.

I'm increasingly uncomfortable living a double life. Ellen and I have grown more distant, and I hate it when I lie to Kelsie or Julie. More people on campus have figured out that Judy and I are a couple, and we're getting settled enough in our relationship to become reckless. So she'll occasionally call the house, and if I answer, we'll make a plan for her to pick me up near the entrance to our development. I announce that I'm going for a walk, she drives us to a secluded spot I located earlier, and she gives me oral sex before bringing me back to "complete my walk."

I'm thinking with my crotch enough not to ask myself what has happened to my commitment to my marriage. But I am at least feeling a little guilty. I decide it's time to move toward less lying by talking seriously with Ellen and the girls and scheduling a separation.

First, I ask Ellen again about us seeing a counselor, and she continues to resist. Unfortunately, her discomfort provides me with a level of self-righteousness that I haven't earned—"Well, I've done everything I could …" My lurch down the road toward divorce is also supported by a colleague who split from his wife three years before and who insists that their son is doing well.

I work to persuade Ellen that the problems that we have can't be solved, that even after she's a dental hygienist, we still won't be happy with each other. I say nothing about Judy. I tell Ellen I think that it will be best for the girls to live with her, so long as I can spend time with them frequently. I agree to let her have the house. I also promise to provide child support and to use royalty income to build college funds for the girls.

I propose that we find one attorney to handle the divorce, so we don't end up fighting each other in court. Not only will this be much easier on the girls, I argue, but it will also keep us from spending down what little reserves we have to pay legal fees.

In April 1974, I write a letter to the local Bar Association's referral service asking to be "put in touch with an attorney who is willing and able genuinely to serve *us* in the letter and spirit of Massachusetts' 'no fault' [divorce] legislation." A young lawyer with some experience in family law responds, and our appointment is set for May 9 at 3:00 p.m.

The lawyer emphasizes the risks to both of us if we proceed this way. Each party in a divorce, he says, should have an attorney protecting his or her interests. We convince him that we don't have anything to fight about. I'm obviously eager, and Ellen has resigned herself to a course of action that, I learn later, she feels powerless to change.

The hardest part of the process is talking with Kelsie and Julie. If I weren't so anesthetized by thinking with my crotch, I wouldn't have been able to do it. I tell the girls that their mom and I are not happy together and that we don't see any way to fix things. I've come to actually believe what I've read and been told about children surviving divorce, so long as the process is amicable, and I assure them that they'll be secure with their mom, and that I will continue to support them and will always be in their lives. I'm positive that they have been aware of problems between Ellen and me for a long time, so that my announcement doesn't come as much of a surprise. This is just one of the ways that I'm seriously mistaken. Perhaps my most ironic—in hindsight—action is to create a wall hanging for each daughter to put above her bed to help guide her own life. It reads, "It's Always Better Not to Make a Commitment Than Not to Keep One."

In early June, I move into a one-bedroom downstairs apartment below a house a mile away from the university. My bed's a mattress on the floor, but I take pains to set up a roomy and well-equipped work space so I can continue writing the first edition of my coauthored textbook that offers advice to others about how to build close personal relationships.

CHAPTER 6

Married Life 2:
Passionate Pleasure, Permanent Pain

My anticipation of being able to have sex with Judy by candlelight in front of the fireplace in my basement apartment definitely turns me on. I set aside what's needed—a couple of blankets, extra pillows for some positions, candles, massage oil—so they're easy to access. Unlike Ellen, Judy's open to experimentation, and we use her copy of *The Joy of Sex* as a guide.[14] Some positions are more comfortable and satisfying than others, and it's fun discovering which is which. Oral sex is especially good. I enjoyed it with her while I was still living at home, and now we learn together how much fellatio and cunnilingus can add to our mutual pleasure. Each time we're together, it's all I hoped it would be. I do miss the joys of breakfasts and bike rides with my girls, but crotch considerations rule again.

Nobody tries to talk me out of my move. University colleagues and friends have had few opportunities to get to know Ellen, so those who notice the change don't see another divorce as unusual. Ellen's parents don't want to contact me; her brother has his own life; and my family doesn't know how long Judy and I have been together. They have been mollified by my accounts of trouble between Ellen and me, and I suspect they're saying to themselves, "We were afraid this might happen." Mom and Dad just want to be able to see their granddaughters. Everybody involved reassures themselves that "children of divorce are resilient."

So once again I stumble forward, this time dimly aware of some potential downside of my actions but still mainly governed by "the full, tense demand of the erect penile organ."

Judy discovers how difficult law school is, especially if you're a woman, especially if you're a transfer student, and especially if you're still recovering from back surgery. The fifth year of an assistant professor appointment at a Research I institution is also demanding. I have only one more year to publish enough to earn tenure, and if I don't make it, I'm out. So, starting in the fall, Judy and I each spend fifty- to sixty-hour weeks in parallel professional coping modes.

Ellen completes the dental hygiene program, and the divorce is final in December. Judy and I decide to put up a tree at my place and make plans for the girls to spend Christmas Eve with me. We find a right-sized balsam fir at a nearby lot, and as we're decorating it with the few ornaments she's collected and those I claimed as part of the property settlement, we discover a bird's nest in a forked branch near the trunk of the tree. One of Judy's family traditions is that, as she learned it, "If you are blessed enough to find a bird nest in your Christmas tree, happy, healthy, and prosperous you will always be." We take the nest as a sign that our union is special, if not blessed in heaven at least approved by nature. I'm still struggling with what it means to love a partner or spouse, and I latch onto this superficial, serendipitous validation as a partial antidote to my uncertainty and guilt.

This first divorced holiday is awkward for all of us. On Christmas Eve, I make the girls' favorite dishes, and the three of us try to keep the conversation light and positive. My gift for Kelsie and Julie is an inexpensive stereo system I mean them to share. While we're together, they create an eight-track tape of the two of them singing Elton John songs as a gift for me. When they play it, I'm in tears. On Christmas Day, Judy and I attend church together.

I'm pleased to discover that my first book is being widely adopted, and I'm getting several-thousand-dollar royalty checks every six months, with visions of more to come. The percentage of this income that the divorce decree requires is going into the girls' college funds, and there's enough left for me to think about buying a sailboat. It's like smoking a pipe. Sailing, skiing, and a trophy wife will all help me move up the university and the community social ladder, just like smoking a pipe, I believe, helped me fit into grad school.

I'm looking for a boat big enough to cruise in and small enough to afford and to sail single-handed. I find a fifteen-year-old Islander 27 owned by a woman who has municipal moorage, a valuable commodity. We negotiate a deal that includes my being able to use her slip while my name makes it up the moorage waiting list—typically a five-year process.

The first romantic sunset cruise with Judy ends abruptly when I run aground near the opening of the harbor. I radio the Coast Guard, and they understand exactly where I am, because sailboats run aground there regularly. The area is well marked on the charts and by buoys, they remind me. When I ask for a tow to deeper water, they tell me that tide is flooding and we'll be free in an hour or two. It's an embarrassing reminder that I don't know as much about sailing as I should.

My colleague Steve is also recently divorced and living in the dream house that he and his former wife just built on a steep lot. The house is a five-level tower with two bedrooms and a bath on the lowest level; a master bedroom, glass-walled bath and den on the second; living, dining, and kitchen on the entry level; a fourth level dedicated to Steve's elaborate office and the living-dining room's two-story ceiling, and a roof-deck. Steve suggests I move in with him both to keep him company and to help ease the shock of his new mortgage payment. I agree, and after a couple of months, Judy joins us.

CROTCH THINKING

Steve is beginning to date, and our living situation has some commune qualities. Acquaintances and friends come and go, sometimes crashing on the comfortable living room couches. Those of us living there have widely varied diet preferences, so we each spend time in the kitchen, have a spot for our favorite foods, and complain about our roommates' leftovers. Every six weeks or so, we throw a party. Most nights, the last couple of hours we're up, Judy and I relax by watching late-night TV and drinking jug wine. After a month of this pattern, I notice that Judy's going through a lot more wine than I am and commonly falls asleep after an hour. Her way of dealing with stress, I figure.

Judy graduates from law school in June. After an anxiety-ravaged bar exam review, she passes on the first try and takes a position clerking for a trial court judge, an ideal first step toward the corporate law career she's decided on.

As I mentioned, I'm dimly aware that Judy and I will get married, and I'm not eager to make this move. I still feel the sting of the divorce, but Judy wants to remove the uncertainty from this part of her life, partly because there's so much in other parts. The strain builds, and after a wine-fueled explosion where she threatens to move out, I agree to set the date in December. Definitely not a healthy way to make this kind of decision.

Judy begins watching what she eats so she can fit into her mom's wedding dress, which is a very big deal to the two of them. We contact a priest, who explains the schedule for the counseling that's required, I make arrangements with a photographer friend, and Judy asks the judge she works for to officiate along with the priest. We design our own invitations with a sailboat theme. It'll be a relatively small wedding with a reception at the church.

Pre-wedding counseling circles around the familiar threats to every marriage, money, sex, and in-laws. I barely hear the priest's encouragement to pay close attention to my future mother-in-law and realize that, in twenty years, Judy is likely to resemble her. Nothing is said about stepparenting or children of divorce.

In the midst of wedding planning, I learn that my tenure decision has been postponed for a year, because I've spent too much of my publishing energy on textbooks rather than research articles. Since I've had almost no mentoring about publications, the textbook/article distinction is new to me. I'm given one year to improve my record.

The tenure decision delay makes me worry seriously about whether I'm a capable enough academic to compete in a Research I university.[15] I figure I'd better investigate alternative ways to earn a living without moving to another city or state, because a move might force Judy to take another bar exam. One option I consider is selling sailboats. I could also teach part-time at one of the local community colleges. This backup planning does little to reduce my embarrassment at failing to clear this professional hurdle the first time, and my fear about whether I'll eventually make it.

A counselor helps me sort out the stress. After listening to me for a couple of sessions, Dr. Chancellor asks me how long I've been riding around on my white horse in an effort to save everyone around me. He's identifying the codependence I mentioned, but he doesn't call it that. At the time, his question surprises me, but I can't deny the truth of it.

I'm most comfortable in my life when other people rely on me because I'm fixing problems for them. I depend on their depending on me. This is one reason why I immediately agreed to marry Ellen, even though I wasn't in love with her. And why I believe I should be the one solving Julie's and Ellen's problems and minimizing the uncertainty in Judy's life.

A second understanding I get from this round of counseling strikes me now as so obvious that I should have learned it much earlier. As Dr. Chancellor puts it, "It's always best to get out of one intimate relationship before you get into another one." Sounds like simple common sense. What I don't see at the time is that getting involved with Judy, just like having sex with Ellen, has little to do with reasoning about what's better and more to do with my compulsion to satisfy erotic demands. It's reinforcement that thinking with my crotch is not really "thinking" at all.

Around Thanksgiving, Ellen tells me that she's moving several hundred miles south with the girls in early December. It's easy for her to find a hygienist job where they're going, she says; she and Kelsie want to live where it's more sunny; and she believes the move will be good for Julie. I'm convinced that she's also moving to punish me for being with Judy. I worry about how much contact I'll be able to have with the girls. Tellingly, I don't make sure that there's a clear plan approved by the court of how visitation with the girls will work after they move.

The day Judy and I get married, my photographer friend is uncomfortably ill and can't find a replacement, so most of the shots he takes are of people's backs. Sailing partner Alan's wife brings her camera filled with black-and-white film, and she becomes our backup. She gets a few good shots of Judy in her mom's dress, and Judy and I together, but the photographic record of the event is pretty thin, much to the dismay of my new mother-in-law. To her, the problem is my fault.

Otherwise, our wedding day is enjoyable. The priest and judge share official duties in front of our immediate families and fifty guests. Judy has a bride's bouquet, and the florist makes me a fragrant lei. A recording artist-friend performs a song he's written for us and serenades our parents with "Sunrise, Sunset." The reception is simple; no band, toasts, or dances. The cake is delicious. Afterward, we return home, and my recently divorced sister and our landlord, Steve, decide to go out together. So Judy and I stay home to supervise Kelsie and Julie. Babysitting on our wedding night? It's not like either of us is a virgin.

Six months later, Ellen writes me that she and our ex-neighbor, the guy who loaned me woodworking tools for Julie's bedroom project, have just been married in Atlantic City. They are moving back to the trilevel neighborhood, and the girls are delighted to be able to return to their old school. I'm surprised, because Kelsie and

Julie haven't said anything, and I wouldn't have thought that Ian was Ellen's kind of guy. Much later, I learn that, shortly before their wedding, Ellen told the girls that she'd never marry him. Something significant must have changed her mind, I think to myself. No consideration of how the divorce might have affected her. I'm just happy that Ellen has found someone else and pleased that Kelsie and Julie will once again be living only thirty minutes away.

Early 1977, I have a new, beautiful, and sexy wife, and my ex-wife is the main parent coping with our daughters' adolescence. Judy is about to earn as much as I do after eight years at the university, and we are sailboat owners. I've just received an invitation to spend fall term as a visiting professor at a university in the Midwest. The prestige of this appointment will help my tenure case a little, and my time alone there will help me complete two research articles I'm working on.

Without much thought about the timing, Judy and I decide to vote with our bodies for the glass being half-full by building a new house. We find an affordable view lot a mile from Steve's place and engage a young architect committed to a contemporary look and feel, energy efficiency, and a small footprint. He designs a two-bedroom, single garage, three-level-plus-roof-deck home for a childless couple who likes to entertain. He tells us to plan for a year's construction.

The contractor begins work just as I leave for the visiting appointment, so Judy is forced to be project manager for the first three months of the job. We learn what every couple who has remodeled or built a home gets to learn—that a project like this tests a relationship. Dozens of decisions affect how the house will look, how much it'll cost, and how comfortable it'll be. Subcontractors seldom do what they say they will. Since we're building on a hill, there are also structural and safety considerations, plus issues like how to arrange for washing the windows on the downhill side.

Judy definitely feels the pressure, and I begin to get an inkling of some disadvantages of marrying a woman ten years younger than me. Our tastes are quite similar, but when something goes wrong or she doesn't get her way, Judy shifts between emotional outbursts and killer-instinct, adversarial attacks. She's also prone to meltdowns when under pressure and copes mainly by drinking.

If I had used some time during the visiting appointment to look back over the past decade and a half, I might have realized that most major decisions I made between 1960 and the end of 1977—becoming sexually active with Ellen, having two children with her, cheating on Ellen, becoming sexually involved with Judy, divorcing Ellen, marrying Judy—resulted from thinking with my crotch. Although this pattern recedes in importance for several years, considerable damage has been done.

For a time, I can avoid thinking about it, because Judy and I are privileged in almost every way. We have graduate degrees, and we're young, white, and upwardly mobile. Professional and social opportunities become available to us, just because of who we are and where we're able to be seen.

Time and money frame how this happens—a lack of time and a relative abundance of money. Judy takes her first position as a corporate law associate in a midsized firm and begins billing the required 2500-plus hours a year. Shortly after I'm finally granted tenure, I accept a part-time position with a management consulting firm that keeps me busy weekends and vacations during the academic year and full-time in the summer. They charge $175 an hour for my time and pay me about half of that. I'm also regularly revising two textbooks; generating the required research articles, book chapters, and conference papers; and responding to invitations for one-week or shorter visiting faculty gigs. I work a lot of hours during the academic year and most of the summer. Throughout the year, Judy works even more hours than I do. I try to stay involved in Kelsie's and Julie's lives, but there isn't a lot of time.

Judy's and my combined incomes move well into six figures, which is more than comfortable in the early 1980s. When we can manage the time, the money enables us to enjoy ski vacations in Vermont, New Hampshire, and Snowbird, Park City, Deer Valley, and Steamboat Springs in the Rockies. We also relish training for and participating in five-kilometer and ten-kilometer runs, sometimes with groups of colleagues or friends. Judy's back surgeon supports her willingness and ability to be physically active; for a time, she's a poster child for his office.

Neither of us is able to handle anything longer than a 10K or much above intermediate ski runs, but we thoroughly enjoy the physical challenge of running, the romance and party atmosphere of the various ski villages, and the beauty of views from chairlifts and restaurants at the tops of the mountains. On ski trips, the glitz and glamour sometimes make us feel as if we're in a movie. Lift-side accommodations are great romantic getaways, and upper-end ski apparel and gear make perfect birthday and Christmas gifts for both of us.

We are also active sailors, on our own boat and as crew on a couple of others. Each year, I carve out the month of August to cruise, and Judy joins me when she can take time away from her law practice. This pattern creates opportunities for me, and sometimes both of us, to spend time with Julie. Kelsie doesn't like sailing, and she continues to keep her distance from Judy. We don't see much of her.

Julie's on the boat every summer, though, often bringing a girl friend along for the adventure. We take *Wisp* into the nearby cruising areas, about eighty miles north of Boston, and some summers we head farther north into coastal New Brunswick and Nova Scotia.

Sailboat cruising provides opportunities for using charts and tide tables to plan passages, enjoying beach fires in quiet anchorages, exploring the shops in quaint coastal towns, shrimping, catching crab, fishing for striped bass, salmon, and bluefin, and lounging in the sun. We also experience some exciting—and some frightening— passages when the wind's blowing thirty to forty knots, the mainsail is reefed, and we're flying the storm jib—or no jib at all. Judy sailed as a teen, so she gets comfortable with the boat almost as rapidly as I do.

Julie also learns to handle the boat in most conditions, tie several important knots, and be an effective first mate. She knows the differences between shrouds and stays, luff and leech, starboard and port, windward and leeward. Her favorite crew member, not so much. Julie's girl friend Sandy joins us during a couple of summers and, despite her time on board, insists on calling the cockpit "the patio," the forepeak "the bedroom," and topsides "the yard."

When Judy and I are on board alone, we take full advantage of the romance of sailing. An evening sail accompanied by good wine is matchless foreplay. A quiet anchorage encourages sexual activity in both the evening and the morning. When there's little wind and we're motoring a long distance, the boredom is effectively chased away by nude sunbathing and sex alfresco. Sometimes we test the limits of what we can enjoy without being seen by ferry passengers or people on other yachts.

These are also years of social climbing. Our blue-collar backgrounds ensure that we never break into the "old money" club, but we find ways to progress beyond the fringes. I buy a tux so I no longer have to rent one, and I indulge again my taste for custom shirts. One Christmas, I surprise Judy with a full-length mink and rent a classic Mercedes limo for our double date to one of the best restaurants in Boston and a night at a boutique hotel. Judy and I build a relationship with a creative jeweler who designs several pieces of bling for us. At a charity auction, we buy a weekend's use of an expensive sports car and drive to visit the girls. Judy finds a stable mate of the Alfa Romeo Duetto Spider Dustin Hoffman drives in *The Graduate*, and I gift her with vanity license plates.[16] The consulting firm leases a new Mercedes for me—it's only a 240D, but it feeds my SoCal sensibilities.

This privileged and passionate pleasure happens at the same time as considerable personal pain. Early on, I naively believe that honesty and openness will help us all, so before we're married, Judy and I set a time with Ellen to tell her the whole story about our involvement and our plans. Halfway through our disclosures, Ellen is so outraged at my betrayal and our lying that she insists we leave. Later, Julie lets it slip that, for several weeks after this conversation, Ellen spends most days and evenings in bed or with the lights out in the den, crying. Her resilience is obviously limited.

Kelsie and Julie react strongly too. At the time, I don't realize that they're early adolescents, which means that they're trying to find an identity they'll carry into adulthood. At the same time, they are both asserting their independence and feeling anxious about whether the ways they're maturing are normal. Their brains are at a stage of development where they're often hyper-reactive and strongly need social connection and acceptance, especially from parents and peers. Like all adolescents, they're best served by a home with clear rules applied out of a strong sense of what's right and wrong. It's important for them to do things together as a family, and they have a special relationship with me that I betrayed when I moved out.[17]

If they had experienced their parents staying together in a loveless condition, Kelsie and Julie might well be happier after divorce. But, as I mentioned, our breakup comes as a complete surprise to both, and like almost all eleven- and twelve-year-old girls, they feel abandoned by me and view the divorce as a personal rejection.

Julie, our firecracker daughter, adopts a tough-girl veneer to mask her hurt and gravitates to the other tough girls and guys in her school. She begins experimenting with drugs and alcohol, a pattern she's condemned to continue for over thirty years. One afternoon while her friends are over, one of them puts his fist through a living room wall. Ellen summons me another evening to "help deal with *our* daughter," who's refusing to stay grounded. I spend the night at the trilevel sitting on the bottom step of the stairs to block Julie's escape route. Ellen's incapacitated enough that the things around the house don't get done regularly, and I'm not there to keep up the outside. Life in their household is disorganized, loud, and unpleasant.

As part of her way of coping, Kelsie earns straight As and gets herself chosen to be high school cheerleader. She also tries to lessen her feelings of abandonment and rejection by going inward and, like many oldest children of divorced parents, attempts to take care of her mom. When she's supposed to be enjoying high school, she spends way too much time grocery shopping, cleaning, and giving Ellen a shoulder to cry on.

When Ellen sells the trilevel, she first relocates closer to her new job, fifteen miles west. Predictably, the girls are seriously unhappy about having to change schools. Julie especially starts acting out more dangerously. One afternoon a couple of weeks after this move, I get a frantic call from Ellen and race to their new home just in time to see the ambulance taking Julie to the ER.

She's overdosed on something she got from one of her new friends, and the ER physician says that pumping her stomach will avoid the worst dangers and might help teach her a lesson. Without much anesthetic, he inserts a tube down her throat, injects saline, and pumps the partly digested vomit into a bowl. Julie is clearly chastened by the thoroughly unpleasant process, but she's stubborn enough to pretend that it doesn't hurt all that much. Ellen and I agree that we've got to get Julie into counseling and to help her find a job to fill her after-school time.

Crotch thinking helps convince me that Julie's wildness is adolescent rebellion that's happening mainly because of her age. After all, I reason, Kelsie is experiencing the same changes in her life, plus the same parenting, and she's not in trouble all the time. I figure it's just a current version of the sharp differences between the two girls that Ellen and I noticed soon after they were born. Nothing directly to do with me. Or Judy and me.

The May before Judy and I marry, Julie insists she can't live with her mom, and her mom says she can't control her. The court grants me legal custody. Julie moves into the second bedroom on the lower level of Steve's house, next to Judy and me.

This arrangement works badly. Julie doesn't like living miles from her friends, and I don't like her much-older boyfriend. She pushes back against most of my efforts to control what she's doing in school and how she's spending her time. Sometimes she manipulates and lies, and other times she screams and shouts. At the worst times, she screams and shouts while slapping and hitting me as I try to restrain her. Sometimes she connects, and people at work ask me about the bruises on my face.

Julie's relationship with Judy isn't strong enough to help much, and I spend too many nights awake in the hall so she can't escape out a window. In mid-June, Julie moves back in with Ellen and Kelsie, and they seem to negotiate a better living arrangement. At least I hear less about their problems.

But Julie continues to struggle at school and to date guys three to five years older than she is, often on school nights. Men are attracted to her blonde beauty and rebelliousness. In some ways, she becomes old before her time, serially monogamous but sexually promiscuous.

Her substance abuse also feeds her refusal to follow rules. Julie's second shoplifting arrest gets her sent for two months to a facility for girls whose parents can't control them, where she has to cope alone with jail-like restrictions. I send her an encouraging and supportive card every day she's there, and I hear nothing back from her. She graduates from this institution increasingly chastened, a bit more subtle, and with her abusive alcohol habits intact.

This beautiful, bright, and out-of-control young woman, my baby girl, also learns from the people she hangs out with how to be increasingly manipulative. She's intelligent enough to identify patterns in my communicating like paraphrasing and mirroring back some of what the other person said in order to show that I'm listening. She effectively weaves these patterns into her talk with me and then exploits how parentally pleased I am—imitation is the sincerest form of flattery, right? This disarmed state keeps me from paying the attention I should to some of her lying and other dangerous behavior.

On the sailboat with her friend Sandy one August, Julie enjoys herself, does what she's supposed to, and tells me what I want to hear. But when I leave the two of them aboard to take the dinghy to shore for a walk, I hear them fishing bottles out of the liquor locker before I'm ten yards away from the boat. When I row back to confront them, I discover that they're both experienced drinkers who believe there's nothing wrong with what they're doing. I wring my hands and demand that Julie clean up her act, but I continue not to see the connections between her addictive behaviors and my involvement with Judy and the divorce.

Kelsie's struggles are subtler, although they turn out to be similarly long-lasting. Her model-student high school years culminate in a legacy acceptance letter from UCLA, which she brags about and then discards in favor of the safer, in-state university 150 miles away. She pledges a sorority her first term and gets sucked into its drinking culture. Kelsie's able to maintain her grades for a couple of terms and then gets distracted by the attention of a guy she knew in high school who's completing community college nearby. Mike's not interested in the alcohol culture of the sorority or in academics beyond the two years of college he's completed. Kelsie likes him enough to use their relationship as one important reason to get her drinking under control.

She also gravitates strongly to his gentle, steady dependability. Before long, they're sharing an apartment, and after several months, she asks him when they're going to get married. Many years later, after their daughter and son are teenagers and their own marriage has ended in divorce, and after her weight has ballooned enough to eliminate her desire to ski or swim, Kelsie tells me that she knew she didn't love Mike when she married him. The clincher, she says, was that she also believed that he was the kind of guy who'd never leave her. Kelsie doesn't say, "Like you did."

CHAPTER 7

Addiction Years

Crotch thinking pretty much gets me where I am relationally in early 1985, and its impact is affecting the lives of people close to me. It's helped convince me that I don't need to worry about how the divorce might hurt my daughters. Crotch thinking has enabled me to ignore the contribution to Judy's drug use of the months of heavy pain meds that were such a big part of her two recoveries from surgery. Crotch thinking has helped me overlook what fifty-five empty Tab bottles might indicate about addictive behavior and the significance of Judy's pattern of passing out after several glasses of wine in front of the television most evenings. Crotch thinking has focused me on the excitement of sex with Judy rather than the significance of the ten-year difference between us, an especially important disparity, given my inclination to be a caregiver. Can either of us succeed in getting me to be her husband, not her dad?

Our yuppie lifestyle eventually forces the two of us to confront several of these realities. One emerges because both of us are eager to exploit the possibilities for entertaining that the new house offers, and groups of graduate students appreciate opportunities to get good food and decent drinks at their professors' homes. We welcome them to the roof deck when the weather's good. The downside of our generosity is that Judy drinks a lot. She usually gets sloppy early in the evening, then talkative and loud, and then embarrasses our guests by passing out.

I'm embarrassed too, and pissed, like most spouses of drunks. I cut her some slack, because I recognize the pressure she's under at work. When I overhear phone conversations she has with clients, I discover how many people who are paying a couple of hundred dollars an hour for legal services believe they can verbally abuse the person they've hired. Especially if it's a woman. I also know that Judy doesn't respond well to confrontation, so I try reasoning with her the next morning and partnering with her to plan work-arounds for the next time we entertain.

But reasonable interventions don't work. She drinks too much at most social events we attend, and I begin to worry about whether people at the law office are noticing her hangovers. I also wonder how her behavior is affecting my professional credibility. I'm encouraged when, after many embarrassing evenings, Judy calls a recovering alcoholic friend who immediately takes her to her first Alcoholics Anonymous meeting and instructs her to attend ninety meetings in ninety days.

The friend also urges me to attend Al-Anon. Judy and I discover that twelve-step groups are active around Amherst; we can choose from over two hundred AA and about a hundred Al-Anon meetings every week. We try several convenient ones, and after she's completed her first ninety, we settle into a pattern of one or two evening meetings a week for each of us, plus additional lunch sessions of AA for her, and weekend retreats or conferences every few months. Twelve-step activities dominate our social lives.

We learn a lot, especially in the first nine months. In addition to AA's *Big Book*[18] and volumes of daily meditations for both programs, we read research reports, case studies, and self-help books that clarify alcoholism's genetic, cultural, and spiritual elements, explain family patterns, and offer suggestions for living clean and sober and detaching with love. I also learn some crucial lessons about my codependence.

Its impact on my relationship with Judy creates my biggest challenge. She wants and needs caregiving, and I want and need to provide it. Together, we engage in a pattern of relating that's toxic for both of us.

One example of what I need to change shows up in a contact I have with her brother a week before we're married. George is an electrical engineering graduate who's also a lawyer. He presents me with a file containing meticulously organized and elaborately detailed records for Judy's Saab sedan that he's kept since their parents bought her the car. The dates and costs of every service appointment and repair are documented precisely. This is one way he has helped take care of Judy, and he makes it clear to me that he's passing the torch. Now it's up to me.

I don't notice at the time what this file and his comments say about this pattern in their relationship. She's expected him to parent her in this way, and he's obliged completely. All I think at the time is that I can handle the task as well as he has. I don't get it that she's taking the role of woman-child, and I'm about to be a husband-dad in yet another way. It's a sure recipe for problems.

I also learn other ways my codependence contributes to Judy's drinking. Like most spouses of alcoholics and addicts, I'm hypervigilant, which means I continually notice details of Judy's behavior and pass judgment on her attitudes and actions. When she's unsteady on her feet, I notice. I monitor how her breath smells. I check how much vodka or wine is left in each open bottle. I track how much she sleeps, and when. I look for wine stains on her clothes. All this close monitoring and evaluation help her feel as if she's living under a microscope, and she drinks partly to reduce the stress.

Part of what it means to say that alcoholism is a family disease, I learn, is that my codependence and hypervigilance have also contributed over the years to patterns of substance abuse that I've helped Kelsie and Julie learn.

For example, early in the five years of her first marriage, Julie gets two DUIs, and the second time, the court requires her to spend thirty days in either an alcohol education program or jail. She's heard on the street that the jails are so crowded she'll be released after a week. So, in a classic effort to manipulate the system, she chooses the jail option. She ends up behind bars for the full month, long enough to lose her job and learn several more sophisticated manipulative strategies from cellmates.

Al-Anon tells me that one of my major challenges is to recognize that I can't control Julie's or Judy's drinking, I didn't cause it, I can't cure it, and I can contribute to it. I need to detach from them with love, the program says, so they make their own choices whether or not to drink. The program says that I have to learn to "Let go and let God," to butt out of important parts of their lives, so they learn to regulate themselves.

Readings and meetings with other spouses of alcoholics help reinforce these suggestions. The program also recommends that I find a sponsor, a male who has learned to interrupt his own codependent and hypervigilant patterns and who will work through the steps with me, so we can support each other. Judy is being exposed to similar insights and suggestions from her AA readings, meetings, and friends.

Each of us struggles with our program. There's nothing erotic about the focus on not drinking or monitoring my hypervigilance, and our sexual activity stops almost completely. I recognize the value of what I'm learning about myself and about addiction, but I can't find a sponsor I'm comfortable with, so I'm only working the steps in a limited way. Judy finds a sponsor, but, I learn later, she has problems completing step four, the crucial "searching and fearless moral inventory" of herself.

After the normal pink cloud period most program people experience, Judy has her first "slip" or relapse. It happens one evening, after I prepare a dinner of shrimp stir-fry and wild rice pilaf, two of her favorites. I stay out of her way so she can bill several hours and then offer her a relaxing massage. I heat the oil, lay towels on the bed, and cue up our favorite Whitney Houston and Michael Jackson music. We're both nude, and she obviously enjoys the music and my slow, alternatively gentle and kneading touch. After working her back muscles, I focus increasingly on her breasts, nipples, and the inside of her thighs, all of which, along with the long dry spell, make me harder and more eager. The oil and the candles perfume the air, and her wetness tells me that she's getting as ready as I am. I bend over to kiss her as I slide into her only to realize that she's asleep. Passed out, actually. She's gotten to some hidden vodka and had several shots while I was getting the bedroom ready.

Up to this time in our marriage, it's the worst rejection I've felt. The physical and emotional impact is crippling. She knew where the evening was going, appeared to join with and encourage me, and then drank enough to pass out. It's castrating; she prefers alcohol to sex with me. Does she even care that much?

Then it gets worse. I've consciously tried to respect Judy's boundaries as a professional, a woman, and a person—and, more recently, to apply Al-Anon's advice—by detaching from how she manages her calendar, work commitments, and health care decisions. When I inspect some prescription bottles she leaves on the bathroom counter, I discover that she's getting pain meds from two doctors in addition to our family practice physician. Since her back surgery gives her legitimate reasons to be in pain, I say nothing about them. But I also notice that she's droopy in the middle of some weekend days and unusually tired most evenings. She's becoming dependent not just on alcohol but also prescription drugs.

At the end of 1985, we've been married nine years, and I can already see where we're headed if things don't change. I don't want a second divorce. We loved each other once; she's the kind of woman I want to be with; and we're both engaged in twelve-step programs that promise help. So I privately commit to the long haul, which turns out to be twenty-three more years.

Besides not wanting a second failed marriage, another reason for my commitment to Judy is that I've learned enough about addiction to recognize that I play an important part in the difficulties we're experiencing. I want to know more about my contributions to the toxic family patterns around Judy's drinking and drugging, and also Julie's drinking and Kelsie's struggles with her weight. I've learned in painful conversations with my mom that my dad was also an alcoholic who hid his disease very well. His drinking helped cause the hypertension and congestive heart failure that led to his death at the age of sixty-nine. This is another way it's a family disease. I know I'm not the central person in all this dysfunction, and I also recognize that I am part of the family system. I want to change what I can.

All this learning is reinforced by the family program that's a required part of Judy's first experience in treatment. This comes after a law firm retreat where, her partners report, she is drunk or drugged most of the weekend. The firm's experienced this with other employees, and their human resources person refers Judy to a nearby residential center for their twenty-eight-day treatment. Her workload is temporarily handed off to colleagues.

Judy eats and sleeps at the treatment facility, and I'm expected to show up most evenings for presentations, Al-Anon meetings, and group or couples' counseling. Most of the events are educational, with an emphasis on the painful practical effects of the facts that alcoholism is a disease, and a family disease.

We learn more about the prevalence of alcoholism in various ethnic groups. Presentations demonstrate that the disease is not only physical but also mental, emotional, and spiritual. Studies show that long-term interventions that treat the problem holistically are the only ones that work at all, and their success rates aren't high.[19] The challenge is to change well-established life patterns that are caused by multiple influences, including brain chemistry, family-of-origin issues, self-esteem, communication patterns, and cultural pressures.

In couples' counseling, Judy and I are encouraged not only to be completely candid about our experiences with each other but also to agree on conditions for living together in the future. She explains how hard it is to live with someone who is as judgmental and hypervigilant as I am. I describe how difficult it is for me to function professionally and in my family when she is drinking so much. We agree—I learn later that she felt she couldn't disagree—that if she drinks again, I'll change the locks. She recommits to her AA program. Nothing is said about her drug abuse or the impact of her addictions on our sex life.

During the long sexual dry spell, crotch thinking surfaces again when I become interested in an attractive, divorced graduate student named Sharon. We've gotten to know each other as I've directed her master's thesis, a flattering extension of parts of my own research into an arena I haven't studied. I've learned about my own research interests by working with Sharon and reading her chapters, and my support and encouragement over the sixteen months of her project have provided opportunities for the attraction between us to grow. As always, I push our relationship sexually. After some interludes of close conversation over lunch and afternoon walks in a park near the university, we've found ourselves cuddling and kissing in my office. In a familiar pattern, I've tried to move to third base, and although she hasn't encouraged me, she also hasn't removed my hands from her breasts.

When we make an appointment for a working meeting at her home several miles from campus, I fantasize about the possibilities. We spend enough time on her thesis to legitimize our meeting, and I eagerly move toward more serious petting. Sharon makes it clear that we're not going there now. Partly because her degree isn't finished, I suppose, she doesn't close off future possibilities. But she's not willing to jump in bed with me just yet. I push "control save" and plan to restart my efforts in the future.

One way I know it's crotch thinking with Sharon is that I compartmentalize our involvement so it's separate from my interactions with Judy. She and I complete the twenty-eight days of her treatment grateful for the insights and skills we've learned and recommitted to clean and sober living without codependence. Her senior partners are understanding, mostly because they're used to having to deal with lawyers who drink too much. Their performance standards stay high, though, and Judy has trouble meeting them. Shortly before the start of her sixth year with the firm, she's told to find a job somewhere else.

The rejection is crippling. It's all she can do, with the help of her twelve-step sponsor and friends, to keep from drinking. Judy's learned enough in treatment and meetings to double down on her commitment to AA. She attends a meeting almost every day, and some days one at lunch and another in the evening.

Against all my normal instincts, I try to stay detached from her struggle while still being supportive. It takes a heavy emotional investment for me to keep up with my classes, graduate student advising, and research while watching Judy suffer through the punishing processes of searching for positions, applying, coping with the hard questions she's asked, and experiencing rejection. After several months, she finally finds a corporate counsel position that should be less stressful than the associate and junior partner jobs she's had.

But it isn't. She's practicing a new kind of law that requires knowledge of issues, terminology, black letter and case law, and legal procedures that she doesn't know. She's required to be tutored by a senior partner and to attend quarterly professional development seminars. Because of her history, the corporation puts her on eighteen months' probation punctuated by regular performance evaluations. I unwisely push to have us keep taking some breaks for skiing and sailing, and work pressures mean I go alone part of the time.

Judy's prescription drug abuse worsens. Although I don't think I ever learned all the details, it appears from what I see and hear that her drugs of choice are Demerol with Vistaril, OxyContin, Aminoxin, and Adderall. She uses the OxyContin on almost a daily basis to handle what she says is constant back pain. It also helps with some migraines, but the worst ones require an injection of Aminoxin.

Periodically, she tearfully complains that the back pain is unbearable or the migraine is producing visual auras, so I drive her to the ER. While we wait for treatment, I overhear her telling the physician in a confident, seemingly pain-free voice exactly how many milligrams of Demerol and Vistaril she needs to handle the pain and guard against nausea. It's usually more than what the doctor was planning to give her. She insists that she needs the dosage she's specified. After she is knocked out by the injections she wants, her pattern is to spend twelve to eighteen hours at the hospital and one or two additional days of recovery at home.

I can't help but notice the differences between her desperate agony at home and her insistent and commanding directions to hospital medical staff. The fourth or fifth time this happens, I'm feeling pretty manipulated. She's despairing and frantically needy with me, and much more in control when she's talking with the people who dispense heavy drugs. I feel as if I can't raise this issue without questioning her pain experience and violating my commitment to detachment. So we don't talk about it, and my mistrust grows.

Judy explains her increasing frequency of mood swings by insisting that, in addition to her other problems, she also suffers from adult-onset ADHD. She convinces one of her physicians to prescribe Adderall, and Judy jokes sometimes that her "prescription dyslexia" affects the dose she takes. As she puts it, the instructions may read "take two tablets every four hours," and she takes four tablets every two hours. This kind of abuse means she droops lethargically, slurs her speech, and sometimes even nods off while, for example, at lunch or dinner. During a Sunday dinner for twelve, when she embarrassingly channels Eeyore and then briefly passes out, it's impossible for me to cover it up completely.

Three years after her forced job change, Judy begins drinking again, and after six months of successfully hiding it from me, she checks herself into a second addiction treatment facility. I learn what she's done when she announces that, for the next month, she'll be there every evening and several hours on Saturday and Sunday. The twelve-step meetings obviously haven't improved our communicating.

The family program included as part of this treatment is less extensive, especially for those of us already engaged in Al-Anon.

I learn from other spouses that relapses and multiple sessions of month-long treatment are not unusual, especially for alcoholics with the longest drinking histories, those with compound addictions, and those in the highest-stress jobs. It's almost reassuring at the time to learn that some alcoholic-addicts require four or five experiences in treatment to begin to live clean and sober.

For Judy, the second time seems to work well. She graduates from this four weeks of counseling and care with a stronger grasp of how to avoid the situations and people that trigger her. We agree that we'll keep no alcohol in the house and that I won't order any when we eat out. We ask friends to be aware of our preferences and spend less time with those who feel inconvenienced. We spend more time in church-related activities to balance our twelve-step social lives. Judy's succeeded in learning the new parts of her corporate counsel job and made it through her probation, so her job is less stressful. For two years, life is better.

In 1989, a two-story brick colonial a few blocks away comes on the market. We're both feeling as if we've grown out of the style of our current house, so we make an offer that the sellers accept. The contemporary house sells within a week at more than double what we have in it. With gratitude for the area's booming real estate market, we make the move. Our new home is on an extra-large lot with mature flowering shrubs, fruit trees, and room for a vegetable garden. It also has only one small garage, limited windows on the sunny side, and dated bathrooms. Our equity from the home we sold permits us to plan a remodel that adds a master suite, an office for me, and a workout space for Judy.

About the same time, a former student of mine introduces us to Pine Island, where his family has a cabin. Mark crews for us on the sailboat one summer, and we visit their family's place on the way back home. I don't realize at the time how significantly this place will figure in our future.

The cabin's buoy is in water too shallow and foul for *Wisp*'s draft, so we moor at the county dock, right below the "Two Hours Only

May–October" sign. Mark guides us to the cabin along a narrow dirt road lined with meadowsweet, Christmas fern, bunchberry, and tall spruce, white pine, and balsam fir. We spot their family's wood and glass structure tucked behind a stand of white-barked birch just above a small, private beach. Fragrant azure saltwater, steep green slopes, and rolling hills in the distance dominate the view from the cabin's deck and window wall. Vermont Castings wood heat keeps the inside cozy, and propane kitchen range, refrigerator, and lights encourage serious relaxing after scrumptious meals, drinks, and snacks. Beachcombing, hiking, and immersion in the green quiet guarantee that our time in this spot is delightful.

A long hike the afternoon of our island visit convinces Judy and me that we want more of Pine Island. Half a mile down the beach from his family's place, Mark shows us a cement block structure on a low beachside bluff. Its current owners removed its original roof, lofted the structure, began remodeling inside, and then apparently lost interest.

Chest-high weeds crowd out the old landscaping, broken furniture clutters yard and patio spaces, and bird droppings inside confirm that the place is inhabited by pigeons and crows. Judy's always alert to inexpensive ways to acquire luxuries and climb socially, so she grills Mark about his friendship with one of the owners and his wife. Mark gets us invited to their home for wine and cheese. The four of us agree that Judy and I will clean out and fix up the cabin in return for using it. So we put our share of *Wisp* on the market, buy a used nineteen-foot runabout to get to and from the island, and invest two summers of sweat equity in bringing the cement block place back to something approaching its original quaint comfort.

The owners take advantage of the cabin's good condition by putting it and its hundred acres on the market. When it sells, they give us a generous check for our two years' labor. On the other side of the island, Judy and I find a five-acre place with a small cabin, so we can continue to enjoy island life. By the time construction begins on the remodel in town, we're also using the check we received to expand the cabin there.

So in late 1989, we have two major construction projects underway, a six-figure remodel in town and a similarly extensive but much less expensive rebuild of our vacation cabin. We hire an island builder by the hour for the work there, and I help him each weekend. A local builder and several subcontractors do the remodel in town without my help. For several spring and summer months over two years, we occupy one of the untouched bedrooms at the house in town and camp out at Pine Island.

CHAPTER 8

A Child Won't Save Us

Judy and I agreed before we married that we'd focus our parenting energies on Kelsie and Julie. Now her more stable work life, her sobriety, and her ticking biological clock all motivate her to think about us having a child. I'm hesitant, but I've also made a commitment to this marriage. My determination not to divorce again, my hopeful optimism about Judy's progress with her addictions, and my desire to support her convince me to agree with her that we should try to get pregnant.

We become sexually active again, but this time it's because we have a practical goal rather than mainly out of love or even lust. For several months, we dutifully have sex three or four times a week with no success, so we consult a fertility specialist. He prescribes monitoring Judy's temperature to schedule sex, self-administered hormone injections, strategic sexual positions, and, after these don't work, intrauterine insemination.

The fertility treatments are expensive, awkward, painful, and sometimes humiliating. It's a turn-off to have our sexual activities dictated by her body temperature. We've enjoyed doggy-style or speed bump before, but when the position is prescribed, to be followed by ten post-orgasm minutes of Judy lying on her back with her knees drawn up, sex becomes more about performance than pleasure. Each insemination effort costs several thousand dollars not covered by insurance. The hormone injections are painful for her, and it's impossible to be sophisticated or cool when carrying a cup of warm semen across an office hall to a nurse so she can prepare it for injection into your wife's vagina. She knows what I've been up to. I know what she's about to do. The medical interventions give an impersonal, mechanical feel to what at one time was exciting and mutually satisfying sex.

After months of no success, Dr. Robinson decides that Judy's age—she's forty—and her fused vertebrae make it dangerous for her to carry a child to term. He encourages us to investigate adoption options. Any resistance we might have had has been worn down by months of discouraging and expensive failures. We connect with a respected local nonprofit and go through their qualification procedures. They instruct us how to create a portfolio designed to sell ourselves to a prospective birth mother.

Soon after our portfolio is shown to two women contracted to the nonprofit, the adoption counselor informs us that we have a coffee date at a Wendy's restaurant, the chain consistently chosen for these meetings. "If you ask me where babies come from," the counselor quips, "I can tell you it's Wendy's."

We meet Ivy, a pregnant single mom who has no relationship with the father and doesn't want to raise this additional child alone. She chooses us to be the baby's adoptive parents, and the three of us begin developing an open adoption relationship. We are given access to Ivy's health records and are pleased to learn that she's drug-free and healthy. Ivy and Judy shop for baby clothes, the counselor alerts Judy to a device that will permit her to breastfeed, and Judy and I babyproof stairs, cabinets, the fireplace insert, and every outlet in the house.

When Ivy's water breaks, her birthing partner's car is broken down, so she calls me for a ride to the birthing center. Judy and I are with her through labor, and when the baby boy is born, I'm asked to cut his cord, an experience that hits me surprisingly hard. Unlike Kelsie's and Julie's births, I have an actual part in this amazing process, and I'm helping bring into this world the slippery, squirming little one who will be our son. He looks at me with curious fascination, and I'm floored. I love him already.

Ivy asks Judy what she wants to name her son, and Judy confirms that he'll be Hunter Andrew. During the three-day mandatory waiting period, Judy finds that the almost-breastfeeding gizmo doesn't work very well, but she and Ivy take turns holding, changing, and caring for Hunter, while we cross our fingers that Ivy's commitment to us won't waver. It doesn't. Four days after his birth, in the presence of the obstetrician, adoption lawyer, counselor from the nonprofit, and our priest, and with the video camera running, Ivy presents Hunter to us, and we're parents.

Judy's six weeks of adoption leave give some time for her to bond with Hunter and help negotiate the changes that he creates in our home life. The remodel provides a perfect space for his elaborate crib, surrounded by age- and gender-appropriate décor and some space for toys. We begin a practice of volunteering to host family Christmases so they can be built around Hunter, and Easter dinners include not only friends from church but also Ivy and the adoption counselor. We attend church every Sunday we're in town and sit in the front row, a family display. When he's baptized, Hunter has nine godparents. He's obviously an only child of older parents, at least one of who enjoys grandeur.

Because I've been there, done that, Judy and I originally agree on a sixty-forty parenting split, with her committing to 60 percent of the effort. This is before this little person was wiggling, crying, grasping, and cuddling in our house and in our arms. Now, I'm willing to cut my workload in half to care for him, but Judy insists that we hire a nanny, so both of us can maintain our professional commitments. We spend the last week of her leave interviewing applicants and settle on a newly married young woman from a large family who is experienced with infants, is a careful driver, and has great references.

CROTCH THINKING

Hunter's first three years go fairly smoothly. He seems to achieve such milestones as sleeping all night and eating what we offer just before we give up in frustration that it'll never happen. We enjoy introducing him to the Pine Island place and teaching him about boats, beachcombing, and campfires.

After some resistance, I get used to the grandiose vision that Judy brings to every opportunity to celebrate Hunter. She insists that he have a professional clown for every birthday and to include helium-filled balloons, extensive decorations, special music, a videographer, and dozens of neighbors, friends, and family. The third year, Hunter makes it clear that the clown scares him, and Judy switches to a magician and his assistant one year; an ensemble of medieval knights, damsels, and jesters the next; and then a circus performer with a mobile menagerie of dogs, cats, birds, a miniature horse, and a monkey. Al-Anon supporters reassure me that grandiosity is a common characteristic of alcoholics.

A month after Hunter's fourth birthday, the other shoe drops again. While we are visiting Julie near Baltimore, where's she living with her current boyfriend, we decide to take Hunter to the Railroad Museum, so he can experience its sights, and sounds.

Julie and Judy get into the front of Julie's Honda, and I sit in back with Hunter, who's securely strapped into his car seat. I almost always buckle up as soon as I get into any car, but this time, for some reason I don't. I also don't notice anything erratic about Julie's driving until she runs a red light, Judy screams, "Look out!" and an SUV plows into our right front fender.

The Honda spins violently, and I'm thrown against the door, window, roof, and into Hunter's car seat. Judy and Julie are screaming, Hunter's shrieking with terror, and I'm trying to tell him everything will be all right. Julie is able to maneuver the car to the curb, where people on the sidewalk rush over to see if we're hurt. Judy and I both try to comfort Hunter, and we frantically work to unbuckle him.

First responders materialize with a small backboard and move us away from Hunter so they can carefully transfer him to the flat surface. It's agonizing to see my four-year-old immobilized by straps across his forehead, shoulders, and thighs, being carried to an ambulance with its emergency lights still flashing. The EMTs tell us that Hunter needs to be examined at the hospital, and Judy climbs in the ambulance to ride with him. I hadn't noticed that Julie and Judy each had a paper cup in the car, and I curiously watch Julie dump their contents into the gutter half a block up the street and tuck the crushed cups in her purse.

The police arrive, check on the passengers of the other car, and begin recording license and insurance information from both drivers. When they finish and we're told a tow truck is on the way, Julie and I hail a cab to the hospital.

An hour after we get there, we learn that Hunter's not injured, and the three of us weep with relief. We sign for his release and get another cab for the forty-minute ride back to Julie's place. Hunter's still upset by what's happened, and we all focus on trying to make him as comfortable as possible. When we get back, I watch Julie dump the cups in the garbage. I retrieve them as subtly as I can. It takes only a small sniff to confirm that they held vodka and something.

As usual, I avoid a confrontation. When the realization sinks in, though, I sense that, once again, I'm experiencing a life event that separates a before from an after. Julie and Judy have a long-standing daughter-stepmother relationship that I value in many ways. But it's a relationship that includes at least drinking together and maybe sharing drugs. They apparently indulge their addictions whenever they're with each other. If you believe that alcoholism's a disease, neither of them is willing or able to keep from drinking, even when one of them is driving with a four-year-old, *their* four-year-old nephew/son, in the car. The addictions push them to risk Hunter's safety, and even his life! If you don't believe alcoholism's a disease, it's even worse. It'll be a cold day in hell before I can trust either my "baby" daughter or my wife.

Julie continues to struggle with her own demons. She marries the boyfriend we met on this trip and undergoes three additional treatment programs during her fourteen years with him. The first is three months of counseling five days a week and another twelve months of weekly meetings. She stays sober eight months. A few years later, she checks herself into an all-day, everyday, nonresidential program, and when she again fails to stay sober, they send her to their last resort, a dual-diagnosis inpatient treatment program for depression and alcohol. She finally manages to stop drinking thirty-six years after I moved out and she started abusing alcohol.

Judy's and my road forward is similarly rocky. As I understand detachment at the time, it means that I don't try to talk with Judy about her drinking or drugging, because she'll feel as if it's just more of my hypervigilance. I've got to trust that she's working her program with her AA sponsor. She makes no efforts to have addiction-related conversations with me either. In the belief that I'm practicing the principles of Al-Anon, I redouble my commitment to my program and encourage her to do the same. I drive us to sites of both meetings two or three times a week. I encourage our participation in weekend twelve-step conferences and retreats. I try to reduce the number of family gatherings we host.

When Hunter's six, the parents of one of his best friends invite us to accompany them on a ski trip. After a seven-hour drive to the ski village, we settle into the three-bedroom condo they've rented and relax in the steaming spa nestled in the snow on the deck. The next morning, Judy complains of a migraine, so I leave her in a darkened bedroom, and the rest of us hit the slopes.

Hunter and Luke find a hill that fits their snowboarding ability levels and satisfies Liz and her daughter. I work to keep up with Sam on a nearby ski hill. We enjoy a glorious lunch in the sun together at the hilltop restaurant on a deck with views of snowy peaks fifty miles in every direction. We make it back to the condo just before the lifts close for the afternoon, and Judy's gone.

There's no cell service, so we wait for an hour, hoping she'll show up. The rented condo is in a cluster of forty other structures, and before dark, I start walking the neighborhood, looking for her.

I try the general store, the recreation center, and even the bars. I ask people I encounter if they've seen Judy, and finally run into a man who's looking for someone to take responsibility for an obviously drunk woman who stumbled through their unlocked condo door and collapsed on their couch. He takes me to where Judy's passed out, and after we both try to awaken her, he calls an ambulance. As the EMTs are loading her into their rig, a nearly empty vodka bottle falls out of her anorak.

The ambulance heads for the nearest hospital, twenty miles down the mountain. One of the low points of my life is this bumpy ride, siren blaring, lights flashing, attendant in the back trying to wake Judy, and a grim driver negotiating the curves. Medical personnel at the hospital determine that her blood-alcohol level is almost four times the legal limit, and they pump her stomach.

Sam drives down the hill to pick us up. Judy's too incapacitated and embarrassed to talk about what happened and stays in the bedroom until we leave. She insists that we stick to the migraine story to keep Hunter from knowing what actually happened. We never resume the enjoyable social times we've had with Luke's family.

Judy's drug and alcohol abuse soon get her fired from the corporate law position. Her only option at this point is to open her own office, and she promptly discovers dozens of business startup challenges she's never experienced. She hires an administrative assistant to help with the office lease, furniture and equipment rental, malpractice insurance, payroll requirements, IT design and maintenance, marketing, and other necessities. After six months, Judy finds that her assistant is embezzling funds, and she has to fire her, find a replacement, and decide whether and how to try to recoup what the assistant has stolen. The stress builds, I take over Judy's job of managing the nanny, and I spend more time with Hunter so she can try to work.

For several years, I've wanted to return to the kind of institutional experience I had as an undergraduate. This desire has overcome my worry about forcing Judy to take another bar exam, and I've been actively searching for a position at a small Christian university. An opportunity arises at a Catholic school in the Midwest looking for a vice president for academic affairs. The search committee is attracted by my thirty-plus years at a major research institution and the fact that I'm not Catholic. I'm offered the position at what might be close to the last possible moment for Judy.

She's persuaded a single mom from church to retain her to bring a claim for injuries that the mom's nine-year-old son suffered when he was half-drowned in a private swimming pool. Judy's never done personal injury law before. This will be her first jury trial. It's the only active case in her office. She has grandiose visions of winning a high six-figure verdict and collecting a fat fee.

As she moves through discovery, filing, responding to defendant motions, and trial preparation, the pressure builds. So far as I can tell, she's not drinking, but her drug use is increasing. She's staying late more nights at the office. Her face shows the stress and lack of sleep, and her makeup gets thicker and more obvious. She refuses to listen to any input from me. She's barely making one AA meeting a week.

After a two-day trial, the jury awards Judy's client $75,000. The judge refuses to consider anything more. I don't know Judy's share, because we don't talk about the financial parts of her business, but it's probably no more than a third. It appears that she's paying more than $5,000 a month to keep the office open, and she's been working exclusively on this case for more than three months. She probably doesn't even clear enough to pay expenses.

So in what appears to be the nick of time, we start packing for our move to the Midwest. Hunter's eight, I'm nervously excited, and Judy's completely exhausted and heavily medicated. Ever since the ambulance ride down the mountain, I've been staying married mainly to keep Hunter from suffering from our divorce. I'm hoping against hope that the move will be an opportunity for all of us to make a new start. Both twelve-step programs insist that moving almost never solves a family's substance-abuse-related problems, that "Wherever you go, there you are." But it seems like our only option.

I spend the first year and a half in the new position getting to know the faculty I supervise, other senior administrators, and trustees and learning about topics that I've never had to understand, such as large-scale budgeting, accreditation, disciplinary trends, and new program development. Judy focuses her attention on moving in, getting Hunter settled into his school and neighborhood, learning the community, and exploring work options. To my relief, she decides not to practice law, but she still completes the continuing education requirements to keep her license. Her need to recover and my focus on a new role in a new place keep us from spending much time together.

Drinking and drugging have helped make Judy's health fragile, and this puts her in contact with a number of medical professionals, which opens doors for her to get more prescriptions. We use different bathrooms in our new house, and I'm still trying to detach, so I don't know what she's taking. The pattern continues of periodic late-night trips to the ER for back pain and migraines.

Then she's hospitalized for what turns out to be gallstones, and after surgery, she experiences a seizure that worries both of us. Two weeks after she's out, she has another seizure while attending a campus social event and is hospitalized again. Four months later, a return flight after a family visit produces a blood clot in her leg, and she's put on blood thinners and required to rest with her feet elevated several hours a day.

Our fourth year in town, I travel to a conference in Arizona for three days, and when I return, I find a bent wheel and broken tire in the back of her car. It takes a couple of days of probing to discover that Judy violently hit a curb while driving Hunter to a Cub Scout pack meeting. Other parents there were concerned enough about her drunken or drugged state that they stripped her of her Den Leader role and insisted on transporting the two of them home. She's required to apply to Pack leadership if she wants to be reinstated. Judy goes through this process without telling me anything about it. I learn the story from one of the parents, several weeks after it's over.

Like Julie in Baltimore, Judy's driven while impaired with Hunter in the car, and I find this really hard to ignore or forgive.

When I try to talk with her about what's going on, she presents me with a seven-page, single-spaced legal document she's drafted entitled "Post-Nuptial Agreement." "For valuable consideration, the receipt and sufficiency of which is acknowledged by the undersigned," it begins, "this agreement is entered into by the married couple of David Thomas and Judith Thomas in order to clarify their intent about the disposition of their community and separate property should a divorce result from the occurrence of any one of the events described below in the 'Events Ending Marriage' section of this agreement."

This document's nine "stipulations of fact" describe Judy's "chronic, daily abuse of alcohol," her job losses, treatment experiences, the "extreme marital discord" her alcoholism has caused, her "lying about her alcohol and prescription drug abuse," and my Al-Anon involvement. It notes that she is signing the document "freely and voluntarily" and "with full knowledge and understanding of the import of this agreement." In four paragraphs under "Judy's Promise, David's Reliance" she promises not to drink, abuse drugs, or lie about doing so, and if she fails, she promises to submit to the "Actions to Be Taken" section of the document.

This section specifies that she will "execute quitclaim deeds to the community real property," abandon all her personal property, and execute a general power of attorney appointing me to dispose of her property. She also promises to move out of the house and give me her house keys and all but two pieces of her jewelry. The document requires me to give her $20,000 and her car, and requires her to give up any claim to my retirement and any expectation of alimony or child support. The final page is a document labeled "Abandonment of Personal Property."

I'm flabbergasted. I can hardly believe what I am reading. The document confirms in detail my view of what's happened in our marriage over the past twenty years. But, and this is a big "but," rather than actually engaging with me in sincere, candid communication, ideally with a counselor to help us, she has drafted an elaborate legal document to "fix" our profound family problems. It's like trying to help someone grieve the death of a loved one by giving them IKEA instructions. And yet …

The document shows that she understands what she's done over the past two decades. It acknowledges the pain she's helped create, the "extreme marital discord" that's grown out of her drinking, drugging, and lying. How can I ignore it? She's taking a huge risk. Especially for Hunter's sake, shouldn't I respect her effort and work with her to improve our situation? With all this on the table between us, we should be able to make genuine progress. I resolve to try to keep trying at least a little longer.

I tell her that we don't need to officially execute the document with witnesses and a notary. The fact that she wrote it and gave it to me tells me that she's committed. We both find local twelve-step meetings and continue each of our efforts to cope.

Unfortunately, we don't work intentionally on our marriage. We don't take steps to talk through what the document describes. We don't connect with a counselor or priest. We don't take time each month to ask each other how we're doing.

I'm working sixty-hour weeks, Hunter's busy with junior high tasks and challenges, and Judy's spending time redecorating various rooms in the house, volunteering for the Symphony League, taking classes in the only graduate program available to her at the Catholic seminary, and, without my knowledge, continuing to drink and abuse prescription drugs.

Eighteen months later, soon after we arrive at the Pine Island cabin for our regular one-month summer stay, Judy starts behaving as if she's gone over some kind of edge. I don't know whether she's drunk, drugged, or both, but she seems to have lost touch with reality. She commandeers the golf cart, our main form of island transportation, and overloads it with a bizarre hoard of garden tools, driftwood, tree branches, and litter. She's not around for breakfast, lunch, or dinner and, I learn later, spends her time on the grounds of a couple of unoccupied cabins that are located away from the main road. She brags about digging "a cat hole" to defecate in. At another point, she breaks into a friend's storage shed and steals a box of cheap wine. I try to talk with her, and she refuses to respond. She's clearly violated all the terms of the agreement she drafted.

I reluctantly decide she needs to be in treatment again, and I locate a facility nearby. With the help of a cousin who lives in the area and is in her own twelve-step program, I transport her there for a six-week stay. Hunter and I return home without her, and I consult an attorney to begin divorce proceedings.

While Judy's still in treatment, I tell Hunter that we are going to divorce. He's a high school freshman, and eleven years later, he tells me that he was surprised that I told him while we were in the car, rather than asking him to sit down at home with both his mom and me. That's the way he's seen it done in the movies, he says.

Hunter doesn't remember that she was in treatment at the time. He also has no memory of her bizarre behavior on the island or of her violent outbursts when she returned home and learned about the legal proceedings I'd initiated. He does remember her moving into the mother-in-law apartment in our basement, because he wanted it to be his bedroom during high school.

When Judy tells her lawyer about the postnuptial agreement she drafted, he advises her to fight my divorce request. Ultimately, the two attorneys determine that a trial will be necessary in order to determine the validity of the document. Threats, orders, depositions, briefs, and finally a full-day trial cost each of us thousands and fill over eleven months' time. Not surprisingly, the judge rules that Judy cannot forfeit either the property or the rights that her document abandons. So the postnuptial agreement is null and void. He requires me to pay her alimony until I retire and splits our combined retirement accounts. Since Hunter will soon be eighteen, he is given considerable say about where he lives. He spends alternative weeks with Judy and me until after high school graduation, when he moves into a house with friends.

During these difficult months, Judy and I do everything we can to keep Hunter out of our wrangling, and at least this effort appears to work. When I ask him to describe the effects of the divorce on him more than a decade later, he only remembers that our conflict made his high school years even more difficult than they already were. He gained a hundred pounds, he tells me, between his freshman year and graduation. I obviously knew he'd gained weight but didn't know how much. He haltingly recalls how he decided to become the class clown in order to deflect the daily teasing he suffered because of his weight. Hunter also admits that the new, intimate relationship he is in currently is showing him that he has what he calls "serious trust issues."

CHAPTER 9

Married Life 3: Getting It Right

Nobody who's been there enjoys admitting that it's taken him three marriages to get it right. After my second divorce, I spend a year trying to recover from the stress of twenty years' coping with a spouse's almost continual drinking, drugging, and lying. I also unsuccessfully try to move past my resentment and anger.

It helps to spend as much time as I can with Hunter. He moves from Judy's house to mine for alternate weeks and is as busy as most high school students with a job, a car, and a girlfriend. Good grades don't come easily, so he spends considerable time studying. Although he's overweight, he stays physically active. Swim team practices and meets fill afternoons and weekends part of the year, and marching band practice, drum line rehearsals, and performances at games and concerts require chunks of his other time. I make just about every meet and performance, and I enjoy talking with him about how they went. He's also working at the local Humane Society and brings home stories about a painfully abused ferret, an especially appealing dog he'd like to adopt, and a couple who's never had a cat and can't decide between a Persian and a Manx.

I try to pay close attention to how Hunter, Judy, and I work out our post-divorce relationships. Hunter's especially aware of when Judy or I put him between the two of us. He gets pretty good at saying, "No, Dad. Talk to her about that."

I know that I don't want to be alone for the rest of my life, and sex is definitely part of this realization. AARP publications aren't the only ones I read that celebrate the possibilities for intimacy after fifty, and I don't want to miss out. I've finally learned, though, that spectacular sex ought to be the seasoning rather than the substance of a genuinely satisfying, long-term relationship. My life's hits and misses lead me to hope for the full package—mutual respect and trust, open and honest communicating, no addiction issues, similar values and tastes, compatible religious interests, financial stability, an even, steady disposition, and a mutually satisfying sexual connection. I know it's a tall order, but it strikes me that at least I'm finally not just thinking with my crotch.

For five months, I don't date anyone. Then, one Sunday morning, I notice the remarkable graciousness of a woman who sits a few rows in front of me at church. I've never met Barbara, but I know parts of her story. She was married for over thirty years to Evan, who served as our deacon. A year ago, she returned from work one afternoon to find him dead on their kitchen floor from a massive heart attack.

Hunter and I are at Pine Island when Evan dies, so we miss the funeral, but I hear that the church is filled. I've known Evan from a distance and respect how much he's given to the congregation. Two months after his funeral, I attend the special memorial and auction that raises several thousand dollars for his favorite charity.

At the memorial and in church, I notice how people continue to express their condolences and support, and how Barbara warmly responds with gratitude and grace. They offer hugs and gentle touches, and she returns their warmth with smiles, appreciation, and humble expressions of hope. It's clear that many connect with her for what they get from her as much as for what they give her. She's obviously a classy lady.

It feels a little like high school when I ask a friend for Barbara's email. I send her an invitation for coffee, and she responds that she's not ready yet for this kind of socializing, so I temporarily focus my attention elsewhere. Barbara's work as nanny for two grandsons a few hundred miles away makes her church attendance sporadic, which means we don't awkwardly run into each other.

For several months, I spend time with a woman from work who attracts me with the claim that she's a gourmet cook and turns out to be as good as she says. Our sexual connection is lively, and I think we're having a decent time together until Hunter comments after a dinner I cook for the three of us, "She isn't very nice to you, Dad." I listen to what he's observed, compare it with some strange stories she's told me about her first marriage, and pay closer attention to what happens when she and I are together. A couple of weeks' reflection lead me to the conclusion that he's right, and I need to continue working on my people-pleasing inclinations.

A year after my first email to Barbara, I decide to invite her to dinner. She accepts this time, and we go to an upscale local eatery where we enjoy wine, salmon, and death by chocolate. After two hours of seamless, comfortable conversation, we realize that it might be time to make room for other diners. On the drive home, she breaks the reflective silence by asking, "Why did it take you a year to ask me out again?"

I stop the car, first in the middle of the street and then at the curb. I can hardly believe what I heard. When she has a question, she asks it! She says what she means! She doesn't expect me to guess what's on her mind! For two decades, I've lived with so much manipulation, so many lies, such a continuous need to walk on eggshells that my main response to Barbara is amazed gratitude. She's a little taken aback by my reaction; she's just looking for an answer to her question. This makes it even better. She has no hidden agenda, no disguised motive.

"I was dating someone else," I reply. And then we talk about this for a while. So simple! And, for me, unusual.

This night begins ten months of courtship that's pretty intense for a couple our age. Her nanny work is a blessing to her son and daughter-in-law and a rich opportunity for Barbara to bond with her two young grandsons. The two-hundred-mile drive each way restricts our time together to the hours between Thursday evening and Sunday noon. But when I'm here and she's there, we get to play with texting and email as ways to build our relationship.

This time, I'm the proactive one. I don't pursue Barbara because I learn she's interested in me. I move toward her first. The difference is crucial. I'm not just responding to her hints or invitations but figuring out first what I want to have happen. She obviously has an important vote, but I'm not mainly trying to provide what she needs with the hope that she'll end up as interested in me as I am in her.

In this spirit, I decide one day to make the two-hundred-mile drive in order to meet Barbara's grandsons and their parents, bring her flowers, take her to lunch, and then drive home. Everybody on that end gets it that I'm serious.

After several weeks of as much contact as we can manage, while we're drying the dinner dishes at her place, I take advantage of the openness we have. "I'd like us to make love sometime soon."

"I've been thinking about that too," she says, "and I'm terrified."

"What's terrifying?" I ask.

The intimacy of the conversation that follows is almost better than sex itself. It's soul-special to feel this connected.

Not long after, we recognize that there's no reason for either of us to be worried. She takes my hand to guide me upstairs, and we discover that we fit together in bed just fine. In fact, a few weeks later, during a break in her nanny work, we fully overcome this hurdle when we make love twelve days in a row.

A surprise birthday party thrown by Barbara's son and his wife offers me the opportunity to meet her parents and siblings. She's one of ten kids from a Midwest farm family. They're a fun-loving, beer-drinking, boisterous group who greet me with cautious hospitality. When her mom asks me what I plan to be doing over the summer, I tell her that I hope to be spending as much of it as possible with her daughter. Her dad's a little put off by my cheekiness, but I think they also get it that I'm seriously pursuing Barbara.

Along the way, I learn that she and I are different in several ways. For one thing, I've been around the water all my life. I taught swimming and managed pools, water-skied since junior high, owned at least one boat since I was thirty-five, love snorkeling, and want to get SCUBA certified. She dislikes even getting her hair wet.

There are other differences. I read fiction and nonfiction, and she mainly reads novels. I was raised on in the Northeast, and she's a Midwesterner. I come from a small family in a small town, and she comes from a large family on a farm. Although these might be red flags for a matchmaker or marriage counselor, they turn out to be unimportant. Why? Because I finally solve the love puzzle.

I finally get it that love of a spouse or permanent partner is a decision more than just a feeling. It's a choice, not just a longing; people commit, not helplessly fall into it. Pop culture's been lying to us forever. Song lyrics, sitcoms, "reality" shows, and fragrance ads consistently confuse love with goofiness and sex, and even though everybody knows this, we still buy it. No wonder so many of us get it wrong.

Love is unconditional acceptance plus celebration; I relish who Barbara is, not how I might change her. Love is respect plus desire; I'm awed by her qualities as a person and want us to spend lots of time together in the same kitchen, workout space, and bedroom. Passion and pleasure are definitely parts of it; I want us to be naked together, skin to skin. But so is her taste in furniture and how she handles money. I want to do things for her that I don't want to do for anyone else. I want her to get to know my family members well and to find close friends in her family. Now all of that chapter of 1 Corinthians tracks for me.

One sign of my love for Barbara is that I accept her water phobias without nagging her to snorkel with me. At the same time, her love for me prods her to get more comfortable in boats and on the beach. I spend learning time in her brothers' corn combine during harvest, and she gets acquainted with high school friends who still live in my hometown. She helps me learn the eighteen names of her siblings and their spouses, and I help her remember my cousins and their kids.

Character is another big contributor to our relationship. In Barbara's everyday life, what she says, who she is, and what she does all fit together. She says what's on her mind, truthfully and gently. No lies. She lives with integrity; no two-faced behavior, and as few differences as possible between her public face and her private one. What you see is what you get. Everybody who knows her respects and trusts her. Just being around her challenges me to live the same way.

She's enthusiastic in our sex life, and we talk about what we do together, so neither of us feels either deprived or pushed outside our comfort zone. "I'd like us to make love sometime this afternoon," I say while we're eating lunch.

Another time, she comments, "I know you like that [position], and I'm not comfortable with it."

"Can we make love sometimes in the morning?" I ask. "I know it's not your favorite time."

"Sure," she says. "Sometimes."

Later—"I'm worried you're going to fall off the bed."

"It's time to get some lubricant."

"Slowly."

"That feels really good."

The more time I spend with Barbara, the more I learn what I wish someone would have helped me see before I let crotch thinking propel me into one thirteen-year marriage to a woman I didn't know how to love, out of it and into a second, thirty-two-year marriage to a beautiful, immature, and troubled woman-child, and almost out of this into a third codependent relationship: although I may be hardwired as a male to focus "solely [on] the full, tense demand of the erect penile organ," I don't have to allow this focus to drive me into sexual behaviors that hurt people.

Two months after our fifth wedding anniversary, I write this for Barbara. It draws from my history, expresses an important part of my truth, and honors this person I'm grateful to have as my life partner.

Barbara Marie
Skies can be serene, encompassing azure
Spanning horizon to horizon,
Lightly spiced with white wisps,
Urging outside engagement, play, enjoyment.
Or menacingly roiled gray and black,
Hosting howling gusts, jarring flashes,
Slanted sheets of drench, and
Sleep-denying, echoing explosions.
Similarly,
Saltwater can be gale-stacked several stories
Into howling walls of spume and spray,
Gut-wrenching terrifying,
Prayer inducing.
And it can be almost flat as
Blue-green construction paper on an antique desk,
Barely rippled by ghosts of soft gusts.
It all depends on the mix.
The blend or clash between millibars and moisture,
Celsius and ceiling,
Tide and topography,

DAVID THOMAS

El Niño and the jet stream.
So it goes with two together,
Spouses, lovers, colleagues, friends.
Relationships can be death traps,
Minefields requiring eggshell treads,
Unpredictable, never-tame tussles
Occasioned by holidays, in-laws, money,
Sex, drugs, alcohol, parenting,
Or the color of the sofa pillow.
Two together can require
Constant high alert,
Fear for what might happen next,
Continuous maintenance,
Exhausting adaptability,
Zero expectations,
A packed tool belt of
Apologies, reassurances, plans B, C, and D,
Delicate avoidance,
Strong strategies for self-preservation,
And a thick, thick skin.
Or the relationship can be a gift from heaven,
Soul enriching, joy enhancing,
Supportive, sane, serene,
Needing almost no protective planning
Or girding of loins.
No escape routes or contingency schemes,

CROTCH THINKING

No crafted explanations for kids or colleagues,
No therapist, physician, or counselor on speed dial.
A space to thrive,
To partner in plans, projects, and pain,
To relish and celebrate blessings,
To live the truth that
God is love and where true love is,
God is surely there.
Skies are out of human reach.
So's the sea.
But you and I can choose to be together gently,
Warmly, friendly, passionately, productively,
Growing, learning, extending, enjoying,
Believing each other into being.
And you bring all this to us,
Beautiful Barbara.
Your smile, soft touch,
Patience with my projects,
Your ready willingness to face together
Our fears, worry, aging, and grieving,
To joining our
Priorities, dreams, intentions, joys,
And our loves of family, church, cultures, and the world.
I am blessed by your presence
At the center of my life.

EPILOGUE

Cultural realities dictate that many men who think with their crotches are powerful. But most of us aren't influential film producers, CEOs, real estate moguls, politicians, media icons, sports physicians, or NFL players.

Most men are also not swamp creatures. We're justifiably proud of the children we've parented, female and male students we've successfully taught, coworkers we've mentored, athletes we've coached, charities we've supported, political causes we've championed, and recognition we've received.

When we are thinking with our crotches, most of us are unreflectively living into the cultural identities urged by our hormones and the cultural narratives repeated by our parents, coaches, bosses, military commanders, and favorite sports and media figures. "Boys will be boys." "This is what it means to be a man." We hardly notice the damage we do.

Since the vast majority of us are out of the limelight, our sexual misconduct doesn't make headlines or even prompt concerned conversations. But it does lots of damage. This misconduct produces several kinds of pain and frequently contributes to divorce. And the comfortable claim that most divorced spouses and their children are "resilient" is over-stated. Divorce hurts everybody involved, and the most vulnerable due to age, self-esteem, family history, or absence of support systems suffer the most.

Ellen remarried a man whom she'd told her daughters she'd "never marry." She eventually died from cancer, and alcoholism killed him. Kelsie married Mike, not because she loved him, but because she believed he'd never leave her. After two children and twenty years, he did leave, and ten years later, she's still alone. Julie's sexual promiscuity ended her ability to have children, and her thirty-six years of alcohol abuse resulted in jail time, stints in three treatment centers, and two failed marriages. Judy still struggles. Hunter learned to control his weight, but he continues to cope with "serious trust issues."

Like them, uncounted numbers of women and children feel abandoned, struggle with overeating, or fight addiction and depression, sometimes for decades. Many view their toxic experiences with husbands, fathers, uncles, and lovers as unfortunate but not unusual, as normal, natural, to be expected. And never discussed.

Until recently, the culture's encouraged crotch thinking, and most men haven't figured out on our own what we should be doing instead. There's no longer any excuse. #MeToo and #TimesUp have seen to that. Just like our prominent brothers, we who live under the radar immediately need to become seriously reflective and openly communicative about our sexuality. Seriously reflective. And openly communicative.

ENDNOTES

1. Sara M. Moniuszko and Cara Kelly, "Harvey Weinstein Scandal: A Complete List of the 84 Accusers," USA Today, October 27, 2017, updated December 13, 2017, https://www.usatoday.com/story/life/people/2017/10/27/weinstein-scandal-complete-list-accusers/804663001/; Jody Cantor and Megan Twohey, "Harvey Weinstein Paid Off Sexual Harassment Accusers for Decades," New York Times, October 27, 2017, https://www.nytimes.com/2017/10/05/us/harvey-weinstein-harassment-allegations.html?_r=0.
2. Ronan Farrow, "From Aggressive Overtures to Sexual Assault: Harvey Weinstein Accusers Tell Their Stories," New Yorker, October 23, 2017, https://www.newyorker.com/news/news-desk/from-aggressive-overtures-to-sexual-assault-harvey-weinsteins-accusers-tell-their-stories.
3. Mary Beard, "Modest Proposals," O magazine, March 2018, 114.
4. Bryan Harris, "The History of Sex Education," National Sex Ed Conference, 2017. https://sexedconference.com/the-history-of-sex-education/.
5. According to the Kinsey report, "Parents who scowl, scold, or punish in response to a child's exploring his or her genitals may be teaching the child that this kind of pleasure is wrong and that the child is 'bad' for engaging in this kind of behavior. This message may hinder the ability to give and receive erotic pleasure as an adult and ultimately interfere with the ability to establish a loving and intimate relationship." June M. Reinisch, "Parental Reaction to Childhood Sexual Behavior," The Kinsey Institute New Report on Sex (New York: St. Martin's Press, 1990), 248.
6. National Survey of Sexual Health and Behavior, http://www.nationalsexstudy.indiana.edu/.
7. Reinisch, The Kinsey Institute New Report on Sex, 92.
8. Robin Williams, http://www.great-quotes.com/quote/5365.
9. William H. Masters and Virginia E. Johnson, Human Sexual Response (New York: Ishi Press International, 2010), 196.
10. Ellen M. Lee, James K. Ambler, and Brad J. Sagarin, "Effects of Subjective Sexual Arousal on Sexual, Pathogen, and Moral Disgust Sensitivity in Women

and Men," Archives of Sexual Behavior 43 (August 2014): 1115–1121, https://link.springer.com/article/10.1007/s10508-014-0271-9.

11. Stephen Marche, "The Unexamined Brutality of the Male Libido," New York Times, November 25, 2017.

12. Roshel K. Lenroot and Jay N. Giedd, "Sex Differences in the Adolescent Brain," Brain Cognition 72 (February 2010): 46. https://doi: 10.1016/j.bandc.2009.10.008.

13. Mark Gungor's official website is www.markgungor.com. View his description of men's and women's brains on YouTube at Mark Gungor, "Tale of Two Brains," https://www.youtube.com/watch?v=3XjUFYxSxDk.

14. First published in 1972, this was the book that brought key elements of the "sex, drugs, rock and roll" culture to middle-class America. Alex Comfort, The Joy of Sex (London: Modest Securities, Ltd., 1972).

15. "Research I University" is the classification that, between 1973 and 2005, the Carnegie Classification of Institutions in Higher Education used to designate universities that granted at least fifty doctoral degrees each year. In the 2015 update, Doctoral Universities are those awarding at least twenty research/scholarship doctorates, and RI institutions host the highest level of research activity. http://carnegieclassifications.iu.edu/.

16. The Graduate was one of the highest-earning films in 1967. In addition to making stars of Dustin Hoffman and the folk duo Simon and Garfunkel, it boosted the sales of the Alfa Romeo that Hoffman's character drives in the movie. According to one source, "The 1967 Duetto Spider, a two-seat convertible roadster, was a real beauty: It had a sharp nose and a rounded, tapered rear end, glass-covered headlights, and what designers called a 'classic scallop' running down the side. It handled well, could go from 0 to 60 miles per hour in about 10 seconds, and got 23 miles per gallon of gas." http://www.history.com/this-day-in-history/the-graduate-opens-in-new-york-makes-alfa-romeo-duetto-spider-famous.

17. The social development of eleven- to thirteen-year-old girls is discussed in Michelle Anderson, "Social Development in 11–13 Year Olds," http://www.scholastic.com/parents/resources/article/stages-milestones/social-development-11-13-year-olds; and "Social and Emotional Development: Ages 11-13," https://www.kidcentraltn.com/article/social-and-emotional-development-ages-11-13. Effects of divorce on children are discussed in Richard Niolon, "Children of Divorce and Adjustment," http://www.psychpage.com/family/childrenadjust.html; and "How Does Divorce Affect Girls and Boys Differently," http://yourdivorcequestions.org/how-does-divorce-affect-girls-and-boys-differently/.

18. Anonymous, Alcoholics Anonymous: The Story of How Many Thousands of Men and Women Have Recovered from Alcoholism, 2nd ed. (New York: AA World Services, 1955).

19 American Addiction Centers, "Alcoholism Addiction Treatment: The Signs, Causes, & Recovery Information," https://americanaddictioncenters.org/alcoholism-treatment/; National Institute on Alcohol Abuse and Alcoholism, "Treatment for Alcohol Problems: Finding and Getting Help," https://pubs.niaaa.nih.gov/publications/treatment/treatment.html.